What Others are Saying About this Guide

I was excited to read this new book by Mollie Bartelt, since the subject seemed to align with my own interests in preserving both family photos and family history. It did not disappoint! I am grateful for the straightforward approach, interesting stories, step-by-step suggestions, and numerous resources for finding helpful information. I really like the idea of using family photos to form the structure of my efforts to record family history. This approach somehow makes the project sing for me. I am so grateful! —Cathie W.

Mollie has done it again! Her enthusiasm for saving photos now includes genealogy and the way photos can play a part in putting together your family tree and history. As in her other books, she's got a lot of information in chapters that are understandable and enjoyable to read. The section on "Using this book" is very helpful! The information in the book has been well researched and offers choices, as well as offering other places to find information, including URLs and QR codes. Using the Passenger Search suggestion, I already found my two grandparents' information. It was so good to see that. I highly recommend this book! —Betty S.

I have always been excited to investigate my heritage. I have just been looking for a plan to help me preserve my family history. This book is so helpful in helping me to get started with my family history and my father's story. I have gathered a lot of photos and history, but I needed the help in technology and putting all the history together. This book has helped me sort along my genealogy journey. And I learned a lot about organizing and scanning old photos to help preserve my photo collection. Definitely recommend this book as it has help me so much and given me the confidence to take the next step in gathering and organizing my family history before it's too late.
Thank you so much —Tania D.

Back in 2022, I decided it was time to organize all my photos and memorabilia into an electronic format. Little did I know that what I thought would be an only time-consuming project would become an all overwhelming, impossible feat! At least that was my initial thought process. I started researching "YouTube." This is how I found Mollie Bartelt. I starting watching her extremely thorough & helpful videos. At that point, early on, I knew I needed to reach out to her. It is unbelievable how many options, right or wrong, there are to do this project. This guide is like having Mollie sit next to you explaining all the steps in an easy-to-read fashion. It does not matter where you are in the photo project. She shows you all the "How To's" to make your Family History come alive for generations FOREVER. This book is my saving grace so that my family's memories will remain. —Robin F.

THE PIXOLOGIST'S GUIDE TO OLD PHOTOS, GENEALOGY AND SAVING YOUR FAMILY HISTORY

THE PIXOLOGIST'S GUIDE TO OLD PHOTOS, GENEALOGY AND SAVING YOUR FAMILY HISTORY

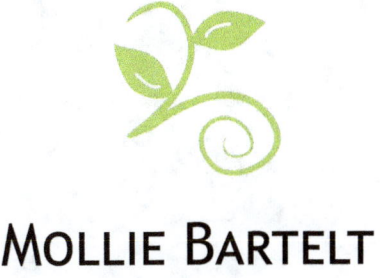

MOLLIE BARTELT

HENSCHELHAUS PUBLISHING, INC.
MILWAUKEE, WISCONSIN

*I dedicate this book to all those who have treasured
and saved their family history along with those
who wish to preserve the legacy of their ancestors.
I hope I can be of some small help in this amazing journey
of discovering roots, stories and memories
through old photographs, treasured documents,
other media and memorabilia.*

HenschelHAUS Publishing, Inc.
Milwaukee, Wisconsin
www.henschelHAUSbooks.com

HenschelHAUS books may be purchased for educational, business, or sales promotional use. For information, please email info@henschelHAUSbooks.com

ISBN: 978159598-974-1
LCCN: 2023945370

Printed in the United States of America

Important Definitions

Pixologie: The study of life through your photos.

Pixologist: A professional who helps individuals organize their family photos into a meaningful collection that is saved for future generations.

Saved Photo: A photo that can be found within a minute or two and has been backed up in two places, one inside the home and one outside the home.

Curate: To pull together, sift through, and select for presentation. We take organization a step further by curating and selecting the best photos for completing a family history.

GEDCOM File: A universal type of tile that genealogists use to move data from one genealogy software program to another.

Photo Estate: A printed or digital collection of photos, film, video, documents and memorabilia organized in a manner that allows another person or persons to view the photos, learn about the lives documented and be impacted by the legacy of those people.

TABLE OF CONTENTS

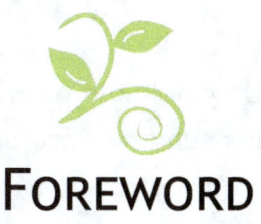

FOREWORD

By Caroline Guntur, The Swedish Organizer

I t was a chilly morning in September of 1997 when I walked into my high school classroom in Sweden and sat down for what I thought would be a regular day. Unbeknownst to me, my teacher had something planned that would change the course of my life—a genealogy project. As the first period started, he asked us: "Do you know who you are?"

We all raised our hands, and he chuckled a little. Now, in hindsight, I get that it must have seemed a little funny that a room full of insecure teenagers thought they had a clue, but that irony was lost on us at the time. "No, I mean do you really

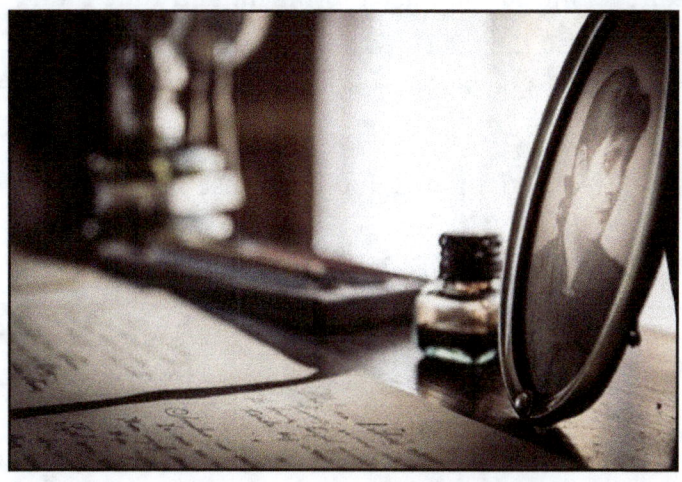

know who you are? Do you know where you come from?" he said, elaborating. "This semester, we are going to trace our family history and at the end, you will all present your findings to the class." Some people sighed, but I got excited. Finally, something that sounded like a cool project.

When I got home, I asked my mother what she could tell me about our family history. She shrugged and said: "Not much. We didn't really talk much about it." Then she turned to me and remembered something. She said "You know what? Come to think of it, I do have something you can use." She handed me a little ticket stub. As I held it in my hand, I realized that it was a ticket to go to America. "Your great-grandparents emigrated to Minnesota in 1892," Mom said. Her statement shocked me. "What do you mean 'emigrated?' Grandpa was born here," I said confused. I remember feeling bewildered as to how any of this was even remotely possible. "They moved back to Sweden right before your grandfather was born, but his older sister was actually born in Minnesota. The culture shock was just too much, and they didn't speak the language, so they decided to come home again."

This revelation is what got me really hooked on tracing my roots. Not because it changed my heritage *per se*, but because I realized in that moment just how much I didn't know.

I also found it fascinating that it had taken less than two generations for that story to fade. What a shame.

For my high school final, my great-grandparents' emigration story was what I presented, and in the following few years, I kept tracing my roots and discovering more and more about myself as I did so. Over the years, my passion for family history morphed into a full-time career, caring for people's memories and leading them to discoveries of their own. I can only explain it as a passion, one that Mollie—the author of this book —shares.

All of us in the "memories" business are passionate, and for good reason. We understand the type of impact these stories can have on a life because we have experienced that for ourselves. In the years that I have known Mollie, I've seen how passionate she is about telling people's stories, and as a Pixologist, she is a well-respected and engaging thought leader in our community. Her commitment to preserving memories changes lives daily, and if that's not inspired work, I don't know what is.

Congratulations on picking up this book! It's the first step in what will be an amazing journey for you. If you decide to follow through, you can expect to laugh, cry, learn, and transform into a more humbled human being than you thought possible. I hope that you will have the same type of life-changing epiphany that I had all those years ago, and that you will also end up as passionate about your family stories as we are.

ABOUT CAROLINE GUNTUR

Caroline Guntur is a Certified Photo Organizer and passionate genealo-gist. She is the owner of The Swedish Organizer, LLC, a company that offers coaching and online courses to clients all over the world.
You can find her at www.theswedishorganizer.com

See the Chapter 13 for Caroline's 10 Steps to Starting Your Genealogy Journey

ACKNOWLEDGMENTS

Many people have helped make this book possible. My book publisher, Kira Henschel, first suggested a book about photos and genealogy and I'm grateful for her support with "The Pixologist's Guide" series of books. We've had fun helping Kira go through her own photo collection, find family history treasures, and preserve them for future generations.

This book wouldn't be possible without the help and assistance of Caroline Guntur, The Swedish Organizer. She is my go-to expert on genealogy and finding the best genealogy researchers. Mary Voell has also helped me understand some aspects of genealogy that I found to be challenging. Please see the final chapter for articles by Caroline and Mary.

I also would like to shout out my friend and Pixologie's co-founder Ann Matuszak whose passion for genealogy has been fun to watch as she's discovered some of her ancestry secrets.

Our team at Pixologie, including Marcus, Corinne, and Hannah, provides me with pride and joy in our efforts to preserve family photos and history. Tyler, our technician, has greatly assisted me in several client historical projects and with advising me on genealogy programs and websites.

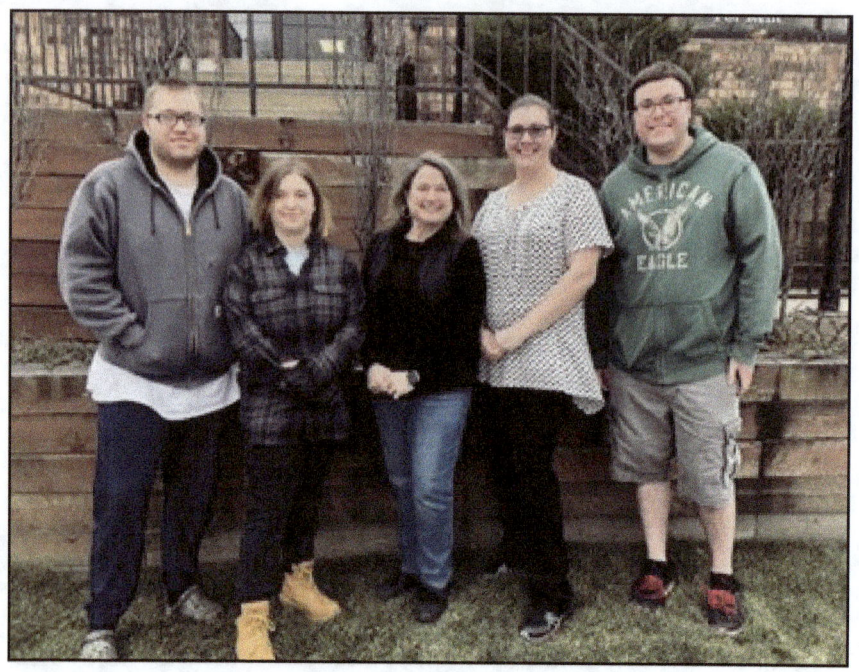

The Pixologie team: Marcus, Hannah, Mollie, Corinne, Tyler

Karen Jones, a dear friend of Pixologie, provided many genealogy insights and suggestions during the review process and considerably improved this book.

My mother-in-law, Eileen Bartelt, has been just a gem on my journey with Pixologie, including helping us at our offices as well as letting me dive into the Bartelt history. Her 90 years of wisdom, stories and her love motivate and inspire me.

And, I must thank my husband Paul, who has been my cheerleader, critic, patient partner, and advisor on my endeavors to help people preserve their family photos, history, and legacy.

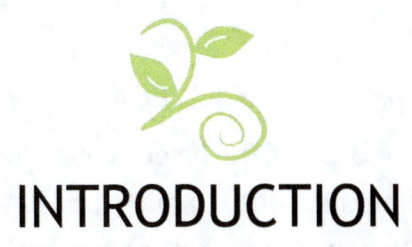

INTRODUCTION

Awhile back, I was able to hold and look at a family bible dating back to 1828. A friend and client of ours, Vicki, showed me the names of her ancestors written in the bible. The handwriting was beautiful old script. One of her ancestors recorded the birth and death dates of the family members. This allowed Vicki and her family to trace her family's roots back to before the 1100s!

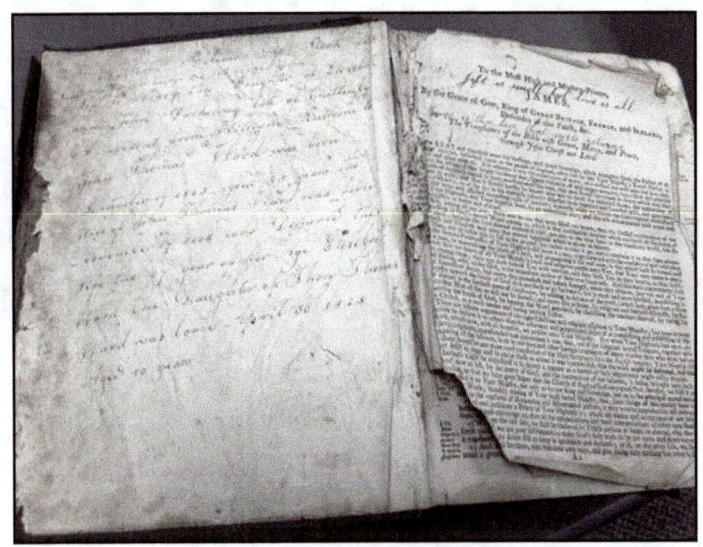

Vicki's 1828 Bible

I am thrilled and humbled by the opportunity to help people save their family history in an age when roots, values, and traditions are disappearing faster than the newest iPhone release. We are at a point in society where technology steals our time, including the ability to make and keep relationships, treasure our past, and plan for future generations. Our phones hold so much of our attention from the latest news, games, Tiktok videos and more. Technology supposedly brings the world together, but somehow, it is pulling us apart at the same time.

It's time to make a stand and save our family legacies using the tremendous number of resources available to us. By doing this, I believe we can help preserve traditions, values, and family stories, and ensure our great-grandchildren know who they are and where they came from.

I'M A PIXOLOGIST

Okay, full disclosure up front. I am not a genealogist... If you are looking for a genealogical expert in searching out your ancestry across the world, this is not the book for you. My goal with this book is to provide a different approach to exploring your family history, an approach that may also help preserve your family photo collection.

As a Pixologist, I'm an expert at sorting through your photos and organizing them chronologically. Over the years, I've organized millions of pictures. When organizing photos, I often find genealogical records, notes and much more telling the "who's who" in the family.

Occasionally, clients mention that they are hoping to work on their family tree at some point. Others have actually started working on their ancestry, and I found evidence of it in their collection of old printed photos and memorabilia with handwritten or typed notes.

Because our clients want to do more with their photos and family documents, I often think about the part photos play in the family genealogy. It truly is a natural extension after organizing very old family photos to start exploring more about the family origins and what life was like back in their day.

I recognize that family photos are a key tool in the genealogical journey and that there are answers in the old albums and envelopes of vintage prints.

My goal with this book is to tell you how old photo collections can be a great place to start putting your family history together.

WHAT IS A PIXOLOGIST?

You may be wondering about the title of this book and what a pixologist might be. This is the third book in a series which includes "The Pixologist's Guide to Organizing and Preserving Your Photos" and "The Pixologist's Guide to Creating a Meaningful Photo Book."

Quite a few years ago, one of our dear friends and long-time client, Bob Riley, began calling us his "Pixologists." It grew on us and we now officially call ourselves Pixologists. What does it take to be a pixologist? I think anyone can be a pixologist. That said, I think there are some skills that need to be acquired. Here's a list of our qualifications:

- Knows how to organize photos efficiently and frugally (i.e., saving 25 to 40 photos or fewer of the 100 in a stack)
- Works with all media types found in photo collections (slides, negatives, documents, film, video, audio, memorabilia, etc.)
- Understands what photos will best preserve stories, traditions, and values for next generations
- Teaches people how to organize their own photos
- Offers photo organization, digitization and archival tools that he/she has personally tested
- Assists with family film and video preservation
- Helps create a family photo estate

THE ANSWERS MAY BE IN YOUR OLD FAMILY PHOTOS

You picked up this book because you have an interest or passion to find out more about your family history and want the clues hidden in old boxes and albums of vintage photos. I am guessing it is not because you have an immense desire or need to pull out all the old printed family photos and organize them once and for all.

In my work, I have learned how closely intertwined these two tasks can be. Digging into your family history? Organizing old family photo collections? It actually is quite obvious that the two tasks are related and even enjoyable to do together.

My friend and personal historian, Mary Voell, helps people tell their stories in written format. She observes that people often want to jump in where they think is easiest—online. She tells people, "Go through your own stuff first." And this includes the old family photos. Don't forget to see her section in the last chapter of this book!

Photos generally are stored with many more items, including certificates, diplomas, letters, film, and many other types of memorabilia. You can see how natural it is that these subjects go hand in hand.

I've noticed over the years that clients tend to treat these as two separate tasks. When organizing photos, many don't even think about the family history side of the project. They just are tired of having boxes and albums of old photos around the house. They are surprised to learn what treasures are contained in their photo collections.

I love finding clues in collections of old photos that clients bring to us. When sharing these clues, we often surprise clients with what we have found. From old Civil War documents to handwritten letters with historical significance, photo collections are a treasure trove for your genealogical journey!

I want to share the excitement we've all had when finding these pieces of history in family photo collections. This book is perfect for:

- People who've never started their family history and are looking for a beginning point
- People who have tons of old family photos and documents and who wish to have a system to organize and save them
- People looking to combine their current genealogy with their old family photo collections

- People who need a quick overview of the photo organizing and genealogy tools available

A LITTLE BIT ABOUT TECHNOLOGY

Over the past thirty years, I have watched the technological revolution roll into our lives. I remember our first Texas Instrument desktop computer in the 1980s when I wasn't even in high school yet. I remember when the blue screen meant you were typing a Word document. I never could have dreamed how quickly technology would overtake our lifestyles.

Today, 81 percent of adults in the United States carry a smartphone (1), giving you access to just about anything you want around the world. There are thousands of apps available. Wearable technology allows us to track fitness and health information directly and instantly as we move. DNA tests help people pinpoint with staggering accuracy if someone you've never met is a blood relative. Someday, everyone's family genome history will be mapped out on the Internet, demonstrating how closely we are all related. (2)

I love what technology makes possible in the world. However, I firmly believe that technology has far surpassed the human ability to keep up with it. I have helped thousands of clients with their computers and phones. I estimate that 95 percent of them are using the bare minimum features with their phones and computers. People don't have the time or technical skills to learn and use their devices. I have also seen clients who don't know to use the Internet to search for answers in their family ancestry.

Every day, I witness the challenges that people have using their technology for daily tasks. And, the Organization for Economic Co-operation and Development (OECD) published a shocking report a few years back that showed nearly 70 percent of adults had poor, terrible, or near to no computer skills at all. (3) Too often, we learn the bare minimum to get something done on our computers and go no further.

Then, on the other hand, we see people of all ages overusing their technology. In fact, a group of Silicon Valley tech employees started a website called "Digital Responsibility." They write to help create awareness of the problems with being over-connected.

Technology does make it very easy to find and share information. But is it too easy?

Imagine that DNA test to find your ancestors. Fascinating to see the results, but who else will have access to those results? Technology and biomedical companies are getting bigger, getting bought out and consolidated all the time. I see a lot of ethical and privacy concerns here.

However, in our journey to find our past, technology offers so many benefits! While sharing the importance of photos in the process, I will explain some of the technology that may be helpful to starting or advancing your family genealogy journey.

WHAT FAMILY GENEALOGY MEANS TO US AT PIXOLOGIE

We love that our work helps preserve family history for clients. But it has personal meaning to us as well.

My friend and Pixologie co-founder Ann Matuszak has been working on her family history for quite some time, using Ancestry.com and FamilySearch.org to track down her family's genealogical background. I don't even know how far back her tree goes, but it's been fun to watch her. While part of an amazing family, Ann was adopted when she was just a baby. She is curious to know about her birth family and has done a DNA test. As of the writing of this book, her DNA test has matched her to second cousins. Over time, she expects more relatives will be identified.

Although genealogy had not been on my top list of priorities in life, I've been inspired to investigate my own heritage. My cousin Kally has spent time with our Kordus family history. I've loved reading what she has found from our massive extended family. I already had photos and documents in my mother's collection to look through. Seeing the stories, photos, and family documents come together has been exciting for my cousins and me.

In addition, my mother-in-law Eileen is 91 and is a huge part of my life. When she is gone, we will lose an important element of being able to tell the story of the "Bartelt" side of the family. We've spent many hours reviewing the photos and identifying people. Even if the family tree is not fully developed, the photos will tell the story of who's who in our family history.

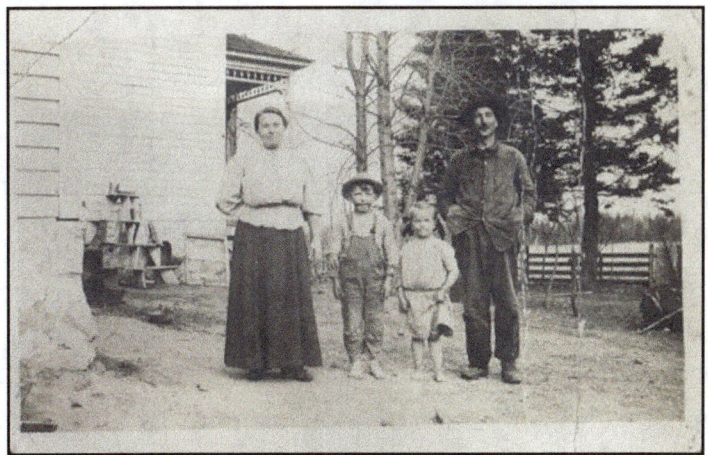

My grandmother is the little girl on her family's farm near Steven's Point around 1912.

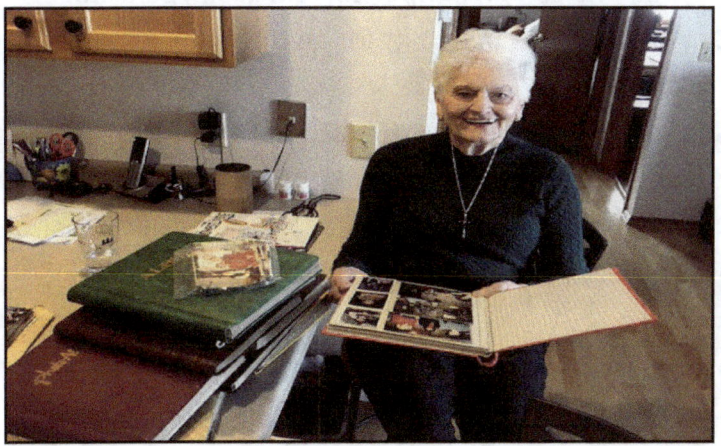

My dear mother-in-law, Eileen Bartelt

USING THIS BOOK

While I hope this book provides you with many ideas, thoughts, even a plan for preserving your family history, I recognize there is a lot of information to digest. After Chapter One, I have divided this book into two main sections:

- Working with Your Family Photos
- Working with Your Family Genealogy

I recommend reading the entire book before tackling the photo organizing so that you can see the entire context of how the tasks related to family photos and genealogy complement each other.

In addition, I have placed QR codes throughout the book for you to use your smartphone's camera to go to related links, videos, and resources that can help you.

For a downloadable book resource list, you can also go to this link, https://www.pixologieinc.com/genealogy/. This document has clickable links for all the websites referenced in the book.

I believe the preservation of family photos goes hand in hand with building your family history records. Wherever you are in the genealogical process, I wish you the best as you preserve your stories for future generations.

CHAPTER ONE

WHY SAVE YOUR FAMILY HISTORY?

Over the years, I have spoken and written about a variety of reasons people need to save their photographs. These same reasons resonate when considering saving a family history. We know that photographs:

- Connect generations
- Celebrate people and milestones
- Strengthen families
- Inspire hope and dreams for the future

Let's talk about how these characteristics apply when saving your family history.

CONNECT GENERATIONS

Obvious reasons to start your family genealogy generally include a desire to connect your generations in some way. We've seen the following situations:

- An 80-year-old client wanted to leave a legacy to her family. While she has no children of her own, our client collected the photos from her parents, aunts, uncles, and her grandparents. She knew it was time to figure out who was who for her family which has grown substantially—down to great-great-nieces and countless extended family. With her knowledge and photo collection, she could trace back three to four generations...but she needed it to be organized, the best photos curated, and preserved.

- A client in his early 60s who realizes he needs to help piece his family history together. His parents are in their 80s and he knows the time is limited to record what they know. His mother is experiencing signs of memory loss and dementia. For her, reminiscing over the photos helps her connect to a past she can remember.

- Another client with children in their 20s thinks it's time to consolidate all of the old family genealogy projects in one place. He also inherited his parents and grandparents' photo collections. In the collection, we found two sides of the family documented and photographed in a variety of ways. However, there was no easy way for the extended family to enjoy, share and preserve the family history.

Children have greater feelings of connectedness and belonging when they see historical photos of their family. Photos prompt family story-telling. In an article for *Psychology Today*, Dr. Robin Fivush from the Family Narratives Lab, wrote that their research shows:

> "... that children and adolescents who know more of their family stories show higher well-being on multiple measures, including higher self-esteem, higher academic competence, higher social competence and fewer behavior problems." (1)

When thinking about connecting generations, consider how much time you have spent sharing old family stories with the children in your family. If your answer is "not enough," then it's time to get working on the family history. The photos help bring those old stories back to life.

CELEBRATE PEOPLE

Old historical photos and documents celebrate our ancestors long after they are gone. In addition, these items demonstrate our values and traditions that some families still practice today.

Look at these examples we've encountered while organizing photo collections:

- A Civil War certificate with a great-great uncle's dates of service

- A very old baptism certificate written back in the day when birth certificates were not necessarily filed with the local vital records department.

- Wedding portraits with dates and notes on the back, helping to identify other unknown people

- Gifts still in their envelopes

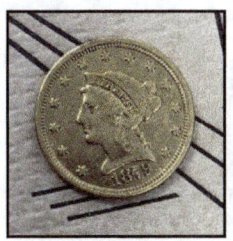 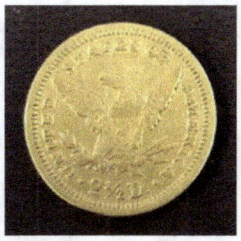 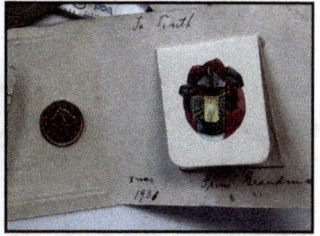

A Christmas gift of a two-and-a-half dollar 1879 gold coin given in 1931 – still in its handwritten envelope, valued at over $200.

- Communion and confirmation portraits that offer familial links to how faith was celebrated back in the early 1900s

We enjoy finding such treasures in photo collections. The photos, documents, and other memorabilia help bring alive what mattered most to our ancestors and honors their history in the process.

STRENGTHEN FAMILIES

Similar to the benefits of connecting generations, I believe sharing family history does strengthen families. We've seen it with our photo organizing clients.

Deborah Gilboa, MD (also known as Dr. G) points out that photos impact the three Rs of parenting: teaching Respect, showing Responsibility, and building Resiliency. I believe this applies to family history as well.

Children today have no idea what it was like to grow up before the 2000s. Can you imagine how a twelve-year-old would function if he were transported back in time to 1960? How about 1940? Or earlier? When we share the family stories of farm life accompanied by a photo, they see lessons of hard work. They learn about how responsibility was given to children in those time periods.

I love thinking about how functional children were when they hit their pre-teens back then. My mom drove a tractor on the farm. Today, we obsess about childhood safety (rightly so, sadly) and have a need to know where our offspring are at all times.

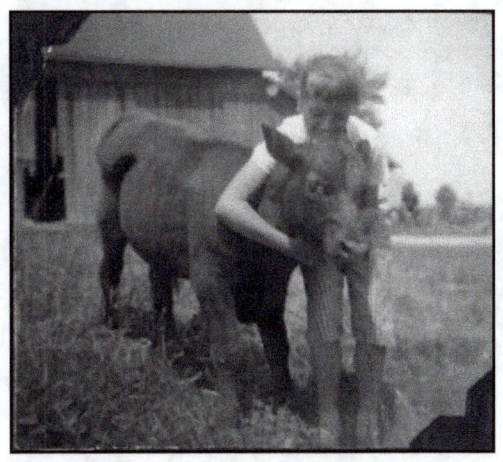

A photo of my mother on her family's farm with her cow Blackie. She often talked about life on the farm, the responsibilities she had caring for the animals and how much she loved it all. She was devastated when her father told her at the age of 12 that the family farm had been sold.

Fivush's research also showed that storytelling with children dramatically improves their well-being. This contributes to better family functioning and creating stronger families. And, maybe our upcoming youth will better respect and appreciate the technology in their lives.

INSPIRE

When looking back over what our ancestors accomplished in building lives for their families, we find inspiration. Consider these items we have also found in photo collections:

- Immigration papers including ship manifests and passports
- Naturalization papers
- Land deeds for property
- Hand-crocheted caps
- 1900s-1930s photos of ancestors working in fields, forests and old machinery plants and foundries

- Armed services documentation
- Travel photos from the 40s and 50s
- Diplomas, report cards

We once had a young man bring in an amazing old portrait framed in the old-fashioned antique glass bubble frame. He was so inspired by the newly found portrait of his great-grandfather from Switzerland, he wanted to have it restored from water and time damage.

Just learning a little bit of your family history will inspire you to take action... to keep digging to find more!

Now, let's talk about the reasons your photos are at risk.

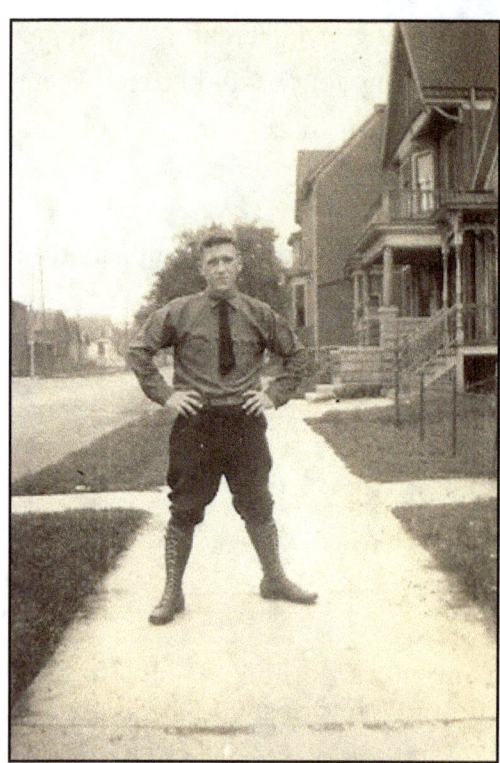

Harvey Bartelt, my husband's grandfather, was a civil engineer. My husband went into engineering and we still have some of his grandfather's surveying tools. Check out those boots from this photo taken in the 1930s!

WHEN DISASTER HAPPENS

When I talk about the importance of saving family photos, I always have to point out that time, disaster, and technology are waiting to steal your memories away.

We watch wildfires consume homes in California or floods wash away houses and livelihoods. Life and possessions are lost. This cycle of weather impacts people across the country each year.

House fires also can strike without mercy. Unfortunately, we've been called to help with a few different fire situations. While in these cases, no one was hurt. But...photos, family history compilations, and family memorabilia were damaged or destroyed.

You can take preventive action to protect your photos by getting them organized, scanned, and preserved. I'll be telling you how to do this in the next chapters.

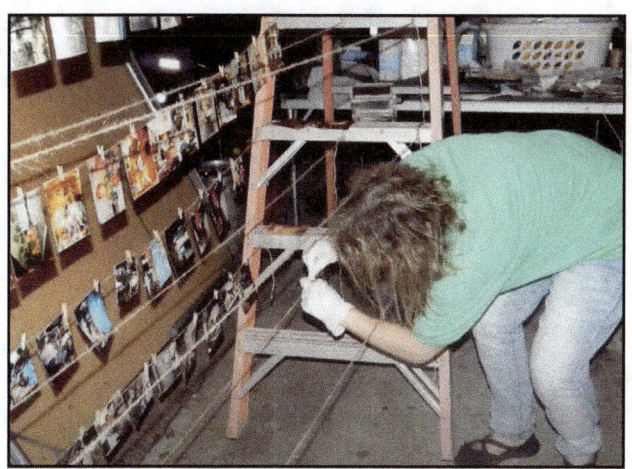

Hanging photos that were soaked during a fire. Only 25% of the photos were salvageable from this horrible housefire.

Another thing to think about: You may have already put a lot of digital work into your family genealogy. Is it backed up properly? Computers and hard drives fail and digital documents and photos can be lost forever as well.

Lastly, time is a thief as well. Before we know it, we can lose the family members who are familiar with the faces and places, the Who's Who and the stories in the old photos. We let time rob us of so much. Waiting really is never the better choice.

In concluding this chapter, I have laid out many reasons why it is important to save your family photos and history. You probably know a lot of this already. Now, it's time to put action to that knowledge. Hopefully, these points will help get you moving on your photo preservation and genealogy journey.

SECTION ONE

WORKING WITH YOUR FAMILY PHOTOS

In this section, you will learn about the methods and tools we use at Pixologie for organizing, scanning, and preserving our client photo collections.

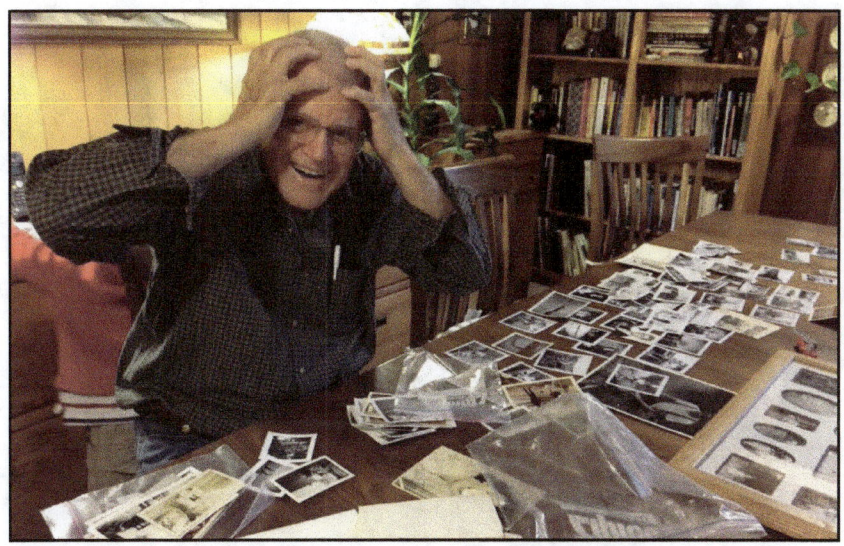

Don't get overwhelmed! We'll walk you through how to sort your photos so you can easily add them to your genealogy work.

CHAPTER 2
START WITH YOUR FAMILY PHOTO COLLECTION

We've heard the saying "A picture is worth a thousand words" countless times. When working with family history, a picture is priceless. If you have not started your family history at all, I suggest you start first by looking through old photos.

And, I would further recommend that if you organize those photos, your family history will come alive in a very meaningful way. For those who have inherited photo collections from their parents, aunts and uncles, as well as grandparents or other ancestors, this is especially true.

Consider these benefits of organizing your family photo collections:

- Find clues to who's who in your family tree and notes as to what was important back in their time
- Match up batches of photos (the 1930s photos are often just as mixed up as your own printed 1990s photos)
- Save space, find what you are looking for with ease

- Remove duplicates; keep the photos and portraits that are in the best shape; find notes on backs of photos that may help identify people in other pictures from the same era
- Marvel at the amazing old documents and memorabilia you may find in those old boxes
- Feel immense relief to have your pictures sorted and preserved for future generations

When we meet new clients who want to have their family photos organized, we find out key details for the important members of the family. Our system of organization includes an initial sort and inventory of ALL photos and materials. Then we dive deeper into the collection with second and third sorting of the photos. We do this in a time-efficient manner.

If you've read any of my other books, you might remember Gen. She hired us with a strong desire to preserve her family historical photos. Her family's photos from the 1920s, 1930s, and 1940s were found throughout her collections including:

- Old, delicate envelopes containing a variety of photos
- Bins and paper bags from several different family members who had previously died
- Photos mailed to her from her brother across the country and from cousins who lived way up north
- Medium-sized negatives mixed up in a fifty-year-old paper bag, beaten up and stored in her garage

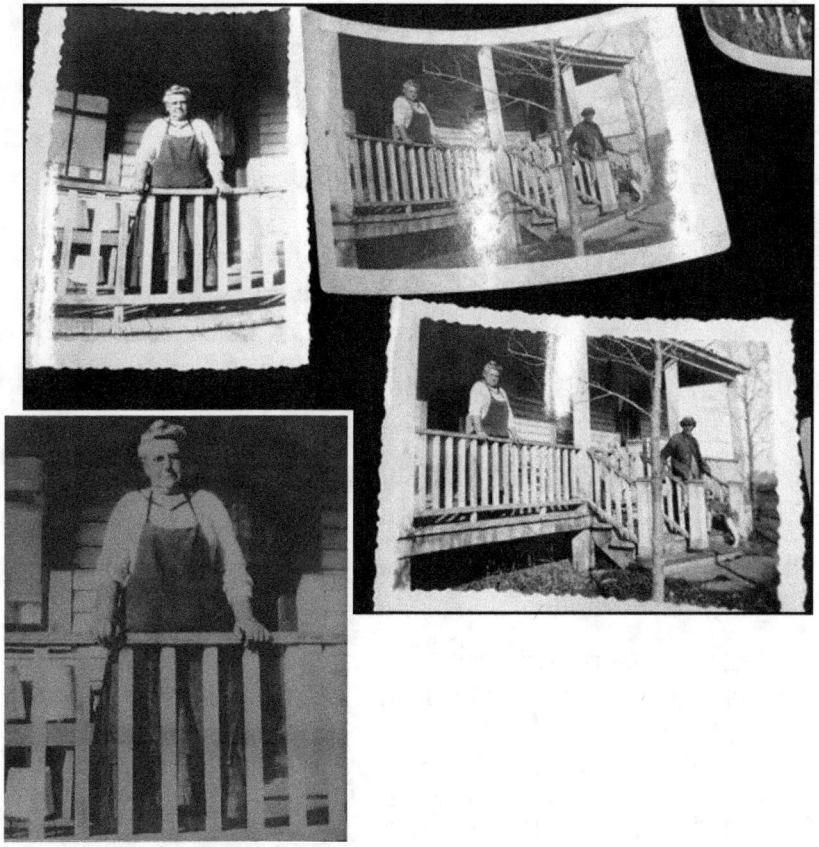

We found all of this in our first sort and set these older photos aside and labeled them "Heritage Photos." It was incredible to start seeing different views of the same event and thrilling to find some of the photos in better condition, even one that had been chalked in color.

As we finished Gen's organizing project, her family tree became vivid with photos and personalities coming through. Next, we took those clues in the photographs and began diving into the unsolved mysteries in her family.

Sometimes previous generations have already done a lot of work with adding photos to their family history. It's possible that the work is not "photo safe." For example, we may find heritage photos:

- Placed or glued in unsafe magnetic albums with handwritten or typed notes of who is who in the pictures. Photos are at risk for damage or may fall out

- Cut into shapes that alter the images from their original perspective—especially in scrapbooks

- Scanned at poor resolutions (See Appendix A for Best Standards in Photo Preservation)

- Photocopied into handmade binders/bound books to share with the family

- Vintage photos reproduced at a local pharmacy enlarged or misaligned cutting off important features of the original print photo

AN EXAMPLE OF USING PHOTO COLLECTIONS TO START YOUR HISTORY

Throughout this book, I'll be referencing one client, Eric, who had a large amount of inherited photos. You can read his full story in the Client Stories chapter at the end of this book.

Here are pages from two albums with the same pictures. Eric's mother and aunts, many years ago, put together the albums for the "Wilson Family History." They reprinted over 800 photos and made at least three sets of two photo albums with the reprints. It was a massive project and the pages of the photo albums were numbered. They typed an index of the

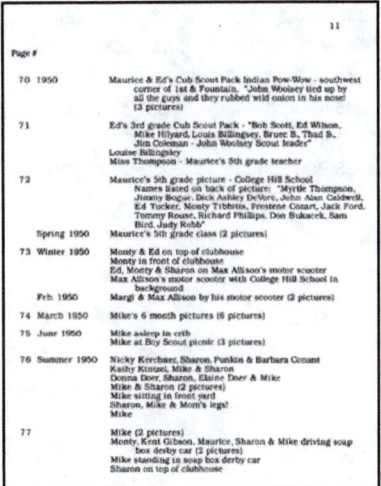
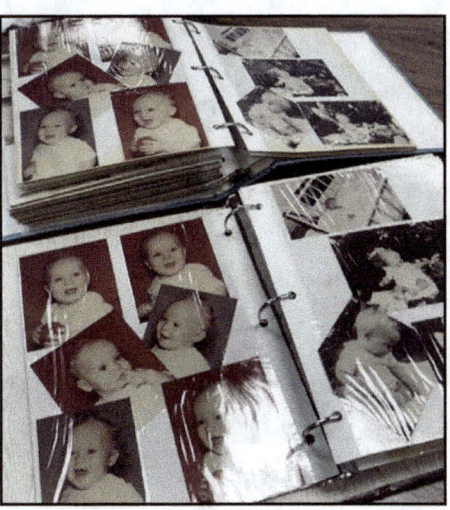

pages and wrote who was who in each picture. It was an amazing project and so much history was preserved.

A COUPLE OF OBSERVATIONS:

- By the time Eric inherited the albums, the three sets of albums were no longer exact duplicates. You can see in the photo that page 74 is at the end of one album and at the beginning of the next album. We had to compare each page to make sure that we had one copy of each photo, and that it matched the index they created.

- The albums mostly contained reprints which were 4 x 6 and either were trimmed or portions of the photo were not included in the reprint. Eric did not have the originals so we could not scan them.

- Pages were added to several of the books that had no explanations and some of the albums were missing pages.

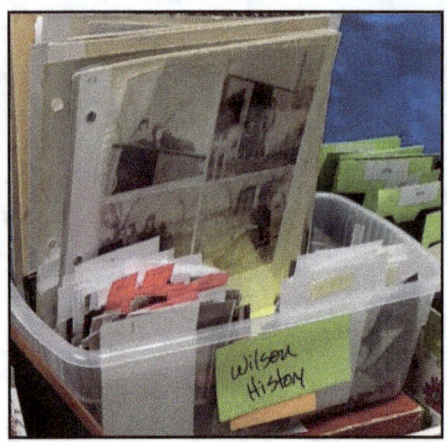

In this photo, you can see we have white note cards and pink stickies to mark each page's photos. The album pages in the back were saved because the photos were stuck to the pages and required flatbed scanning.

Within the typed index, Eric's mother's history was extremely well documented. After we scanned the photos, we uploaded them to a FOREVER® online photo archive. Then, we added the description to the photo's information. See below for an example. This photo was on page 75 and it was simple to add the description and change the date.

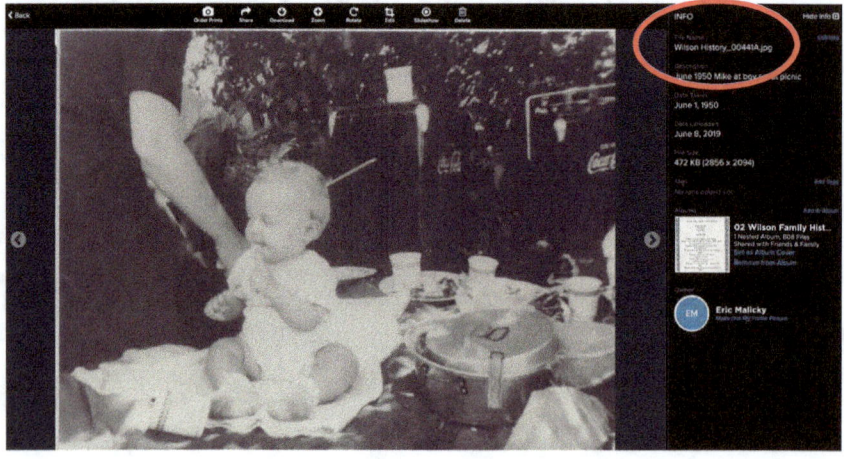

You can see the uploaded photo is a 4 x 6 reprint so the photo is missing its original dimensions. However, when original photos are no longer available, it is great to still have the reprint. Just look at those Coca Cola picnic coolers! How cool is that?

Eric's family has a treasure trove of information in those photos and their descriptions. And they didn't have to do an Internet search to get started, thanks to the work his mother and aunts completed decades ago.

What's in your photo collection that can help make your genealogical journey easier? Let's find out what the possibilities are in the next chapter.

CHAPTER 3
A QUICK PRIMER ON WHAT YOU MIGHT FIND

Your old boxes and albums of photos may cover ten or more decades of family history—maybe even going back to Civil War times.

In the first half of the 1800s, inventors created processes to produce photos using a variety of techniques. If you have such photos, knowing which type you have can help date the photo. You are fortunate to have these in your possession.

To help date photos, I often consult David Cycleback's book, *Judging the Authenticity of Photographs.* (1) Cycleback writes,

> "For family photography, the first photos were created as ambrotypes, daguerreotypes, and tintypes. These are not photographic prints. Instead, the process included making a negative image on a solid plate of metal or glass and that is the final product. Due to a special black backing, the image appears to the viewer to be positive tonally."

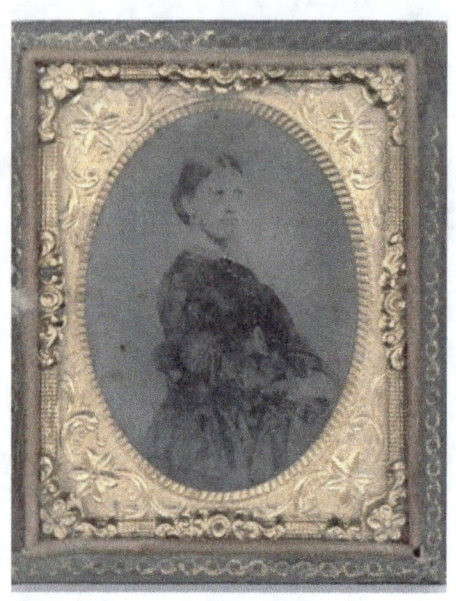

A daguerreotype

DAGUERREOTYPES

Considered the first practical photograph, daguerreotypes were invented in 1839 and used through 1860.

Description: they are highly detailed images on a sheet of copper plated with a thin coat of silver and they are susceptible to tarnishing or having a bluish tint. Daguerreotypes can only be viewed at certain angles, so you may have to tilt it back and forth to see it. Some people describe them as having an almost magical, mirror-like quality. (2)

AMBROTYPES

These were used beginning in 1854 through the 1860s.

Description: A direct image photograph that is an underexposed thin collodian glass negative with dark material placed behind it. These types of photographs do not tarnish but the black paint can crack. The emulsion can also turn dark, making the image appear dark. They often appear to have a three-dimensional effect. In the 1850s, darker glass was used. (3)

Both daguerreotypes and ambrotypes were put in special cases, making them difficult to tell apart. While you can remove the photos from the encasement, be sure to never attempt to remove the photo from the glass.

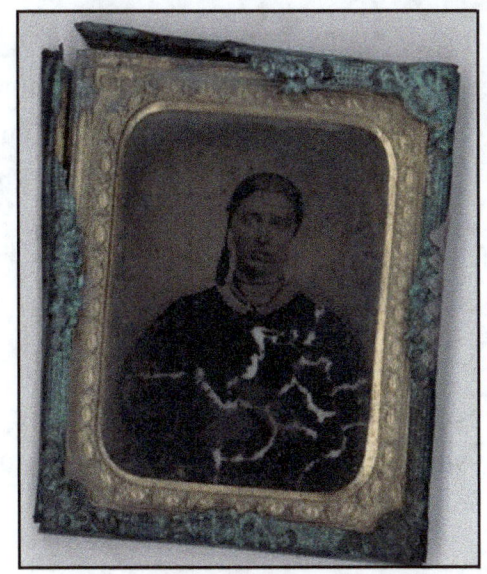

An ambrotype

TINTYPES

These were used beginning in 1860 through the 1900s. They were popular at fairs and circuses because they were quick to make.

Description: The images are flat and on thin iron plates resembling tin. You can find them cut in unusual shapes as often photographers used the pieces left over from prior photographs. They usually are not found in cases.

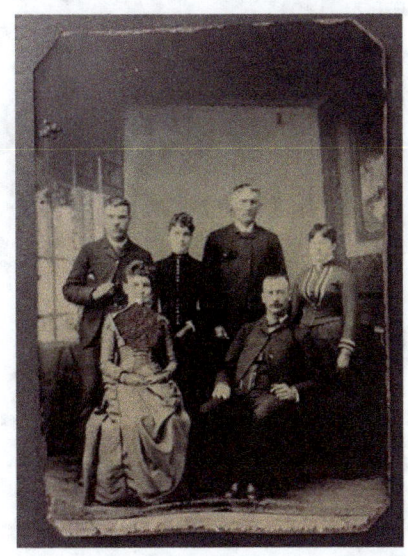

A tintype

The next type of old photographs were produced as cards including the *carte de visite*, cabinet card, stereoview, Kodak card, boudoir card, postcards and more.

For our purposes, I'll cover the *cartes de visite*, cabinet cards, and postcards—the most common types of old photo cards we find in collections.

You'll notice in most of these old photos, people are not smiling. Cameras took a very long time to capture the photograph and it was hard to smile the whole time. The practice of smiling for the camera became standard in the 1920s.

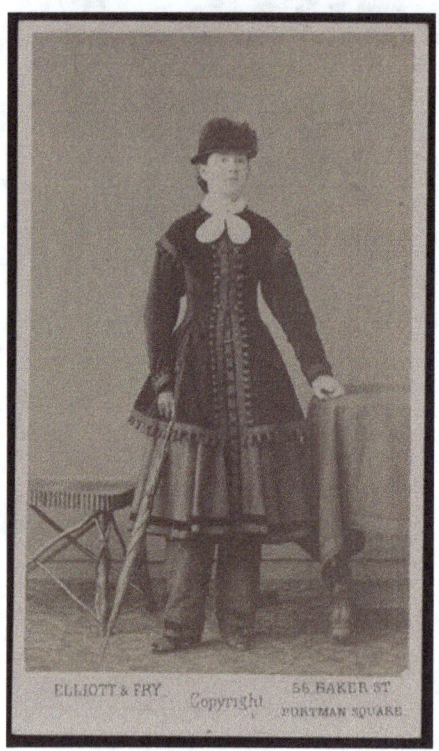

Carte de visite

CARTE DE VISITE

Used during the 1850s to the early 1900s, these were a paper photographic print adhered to a larger card. Typically, their size measured 2.5 by 4 inches. The words are French for "visiting card" and were used for a variety of reasons. Family members exchanged cards, soldiers had their photos taken and even businesses used them. The photo, card style, and printing on the back varied widely.

CABINET CARDS

Again, a photographic print adhered to a larger card, these cards were used during the 1860s to the 1920s. Measuring 4.5 by 6.5 inches, cabinet cards are larger than the *cartes de viste* and people displayed them in a cabinet. There are many variations on the size, print, photo style, matte, and printing.

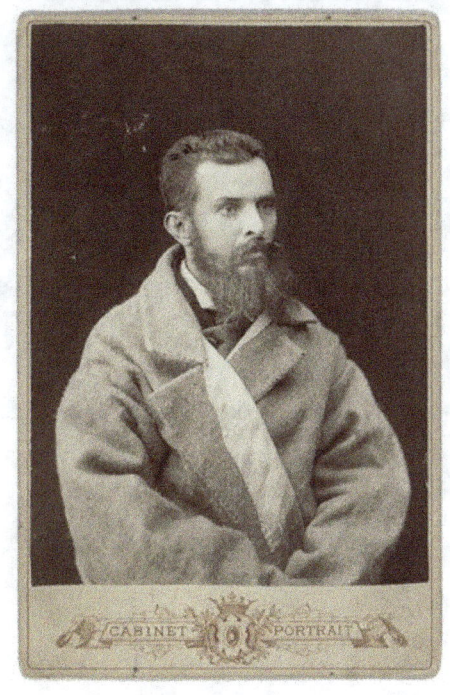

Cabinet card

REAL PHOTO POSTCARDS

Used from 1901 through the 1920s, these cards were postcards with a photographic image on one side (meaning they were not printed with a press and were of higher quality). The US government granted private printers the right to create postcards in 1901. Through March of 1907, these cards were blank on the front panel.

After that, postcards were produced with a divided back for a message on one side and address on the other. Kodak actually sold a postcard camera and people had their photos developed on postcard stock paper. Special stamp markings can also help determine the date of the photo.

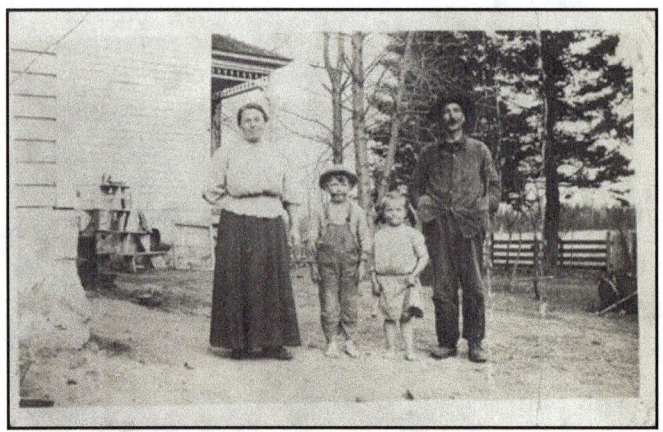

The little girl on this photo postcard is my grandmother probably when she was around two or three years old. The back side of the postcard indicates the photo was printed after 1907 and corresponds to my grandmother's age.

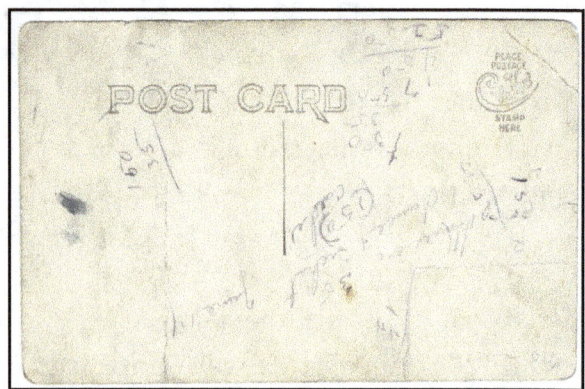

If you have a great variety of vintage photographs that you want to date precisely, consider purchasing David Cycleback's book *Judging the Authenticity of Photos* (available on Amazon.com). He has a wealth of information on the various cards, dates of use and production.

I also like to recommend Maureen Taylor, "The Photo Detective," as another great resource for dating old photos. Her website offers courses on dating photos and many resources. She also offers to date your photo for you. You can find her website and contact information in the References and Resources Chapter at the end of this book. (4)

OTHER DOCUMENTS

Mixed in with albums and old boxes of photos, you are likely to find a variety of documents, certificates, newspaper articles, memorabilia, and more. Here are some examples of what you might find.

LAND RECORDS

From old property deeds to surveys and more, old land records can provide a lot of information. You might be able to confirm old addresses, places of residence, and find proof of ownership. (Please see following pages.)

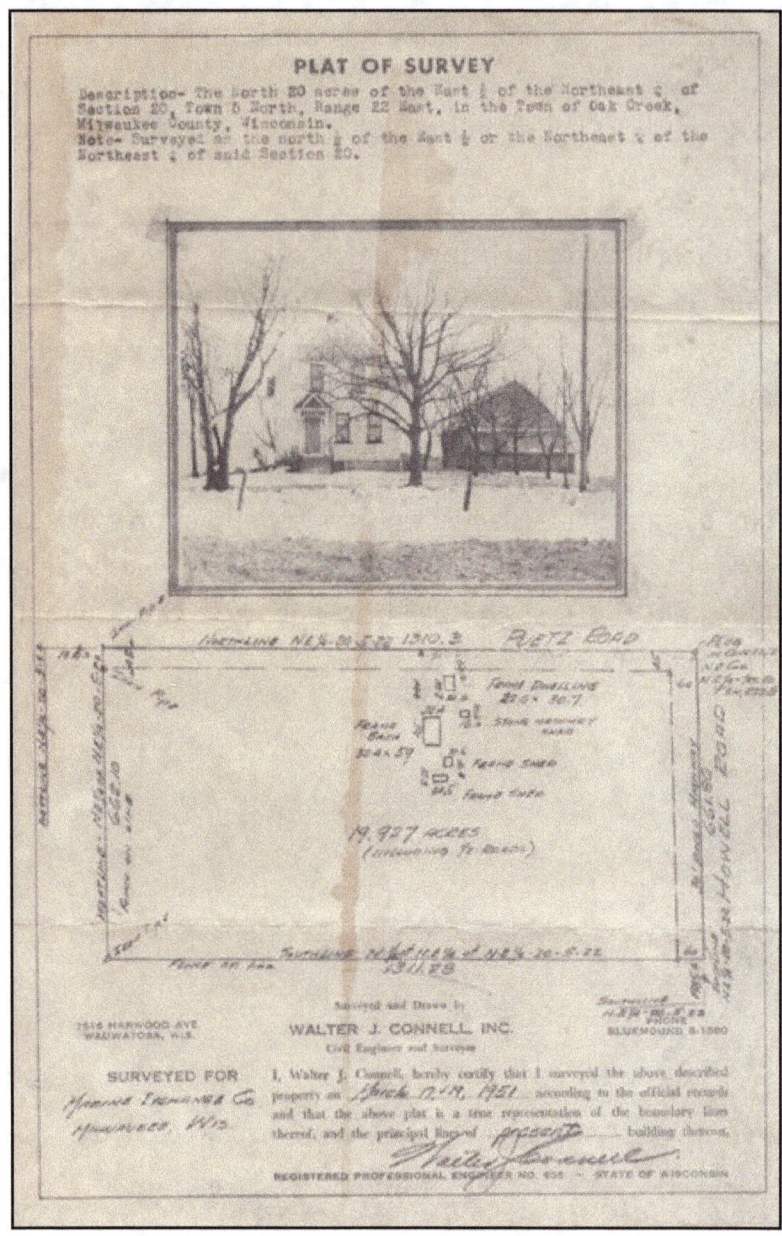

The plat of survey for my grandparents' farm in the early 1950s.
This confirmed that photos I had in my collection were of the family farm.

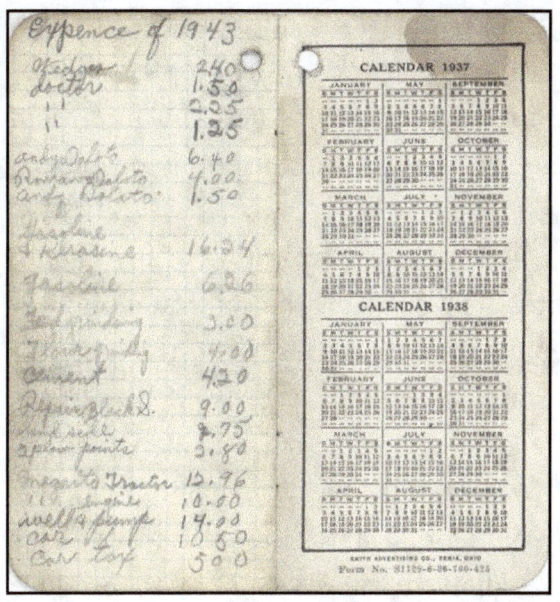

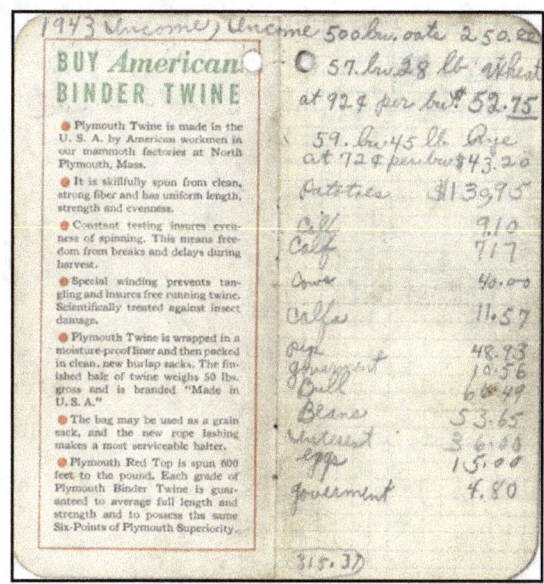

1943 Hand-written Income and Expenses for the farm of one client's family.

Birth Certificates, Death Certificates

Finding original birth certificates provides context, information and a chance to touch history! When you find them in a foreign language, it's helpful to have the document translated.

I was surprised when I learned from one of my clients that US birth certificates, as well as death certificates, did not come into existence until the late 1800s. Even then, certificates were issued by states, so finding records for US citizens born at the turn of the 20th century may be challenging. The US Bureau of Census was established permanently in 1902, but it really took until 1933 for all states to register live births and deaths. This then allowed the US Bureau to produce national birth and death statistics.

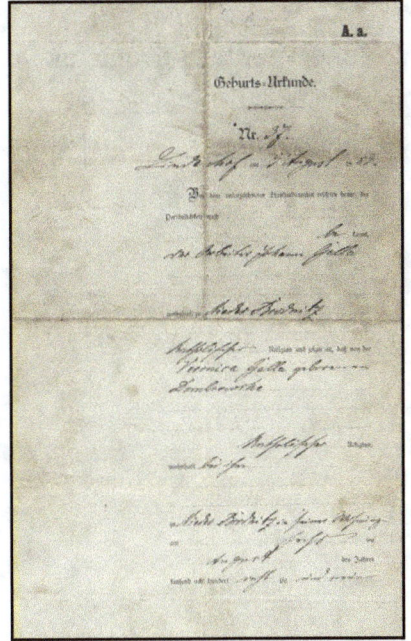
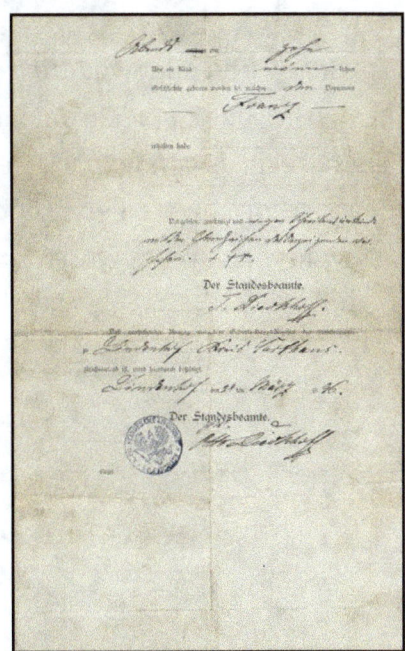

An 1889 Polish birth certificate with its translation.
Written in Old German script. From the Prussian partition.

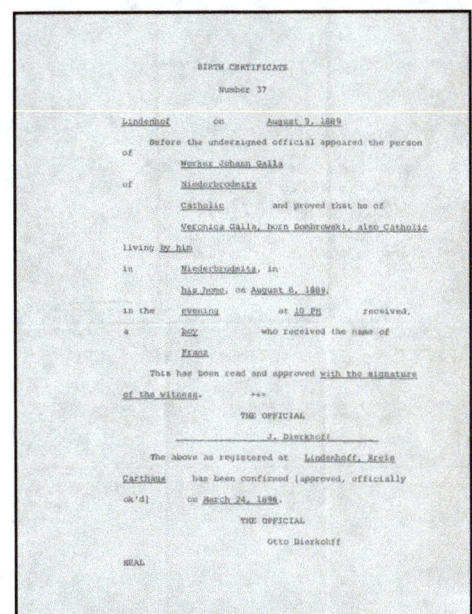

OLD MARRIAGE RECORDS, MEMORABILIA

You may find old wedding cards, documentation and even keepsake booklets chronicling your ancestors' matrimony. These records can go back to the 1800s, long before birth and death records were kept. Older marriage records don't always tell who the parents were.

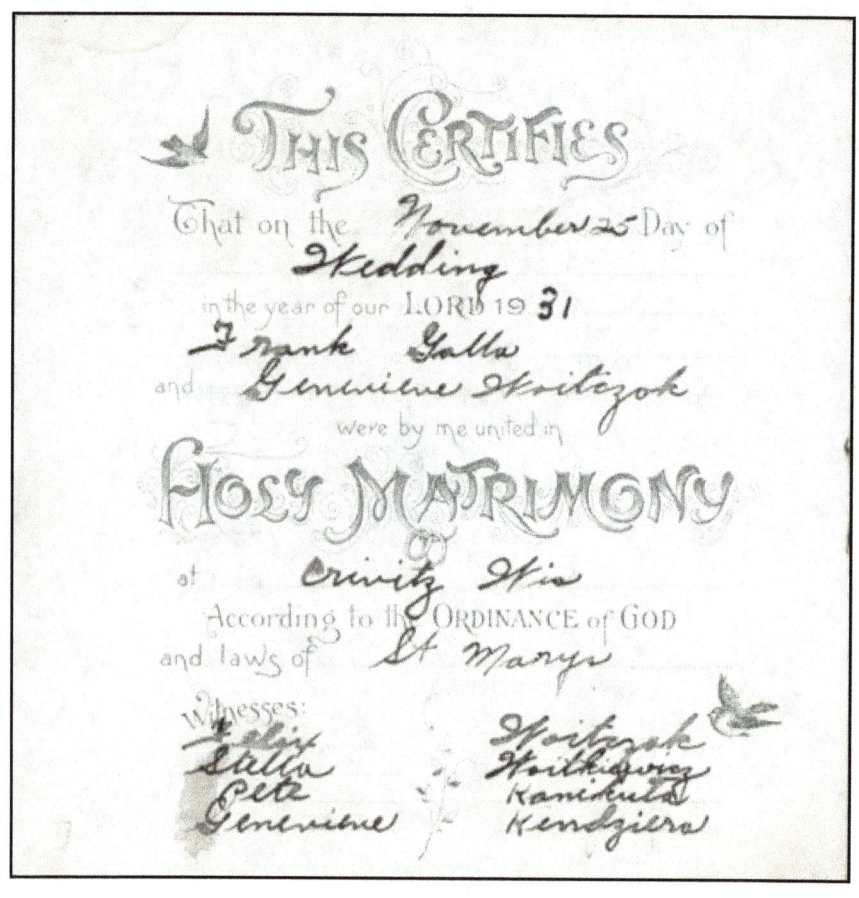

PASSPORTS, NATURALIZATION PAPERS & MORE

It's so exciting to come across documents that tell the story of an ancestor's immigration to the new home country. Often, we come across documents from different locations. For example, one family member, maybe an aunt or cousin, has done some genealogy research. Another family member is the keeper of the photos. When the photos and information are brought together, everybody benefits from further preserving the story.

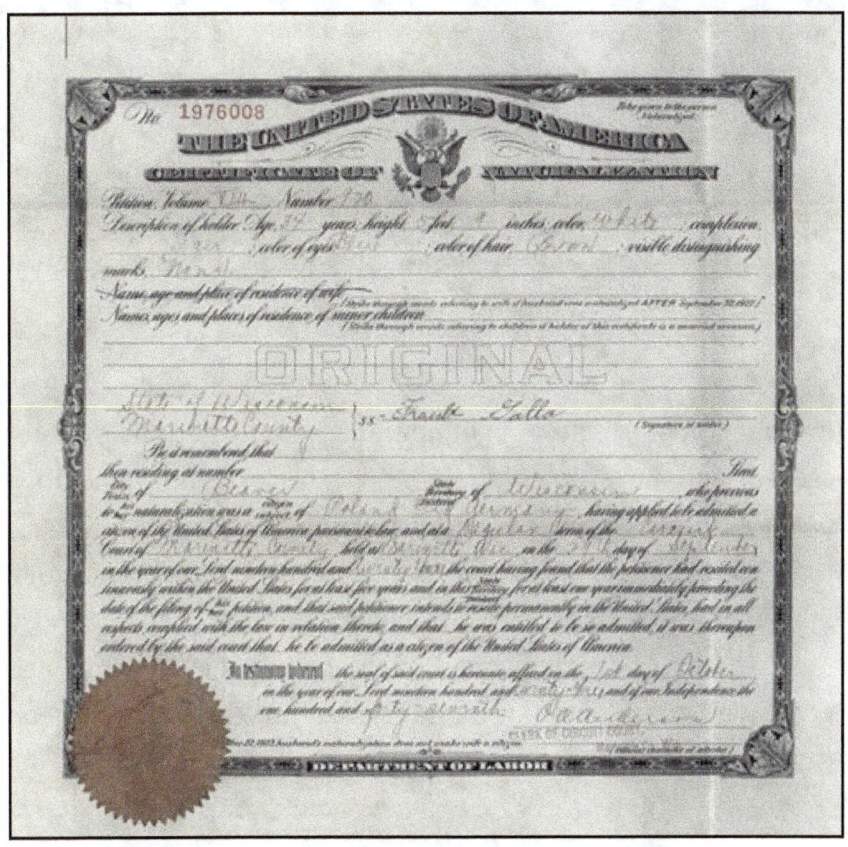

Heinrich Hartmann - Naturalization certificate for my grandfather.
My cousin had this!

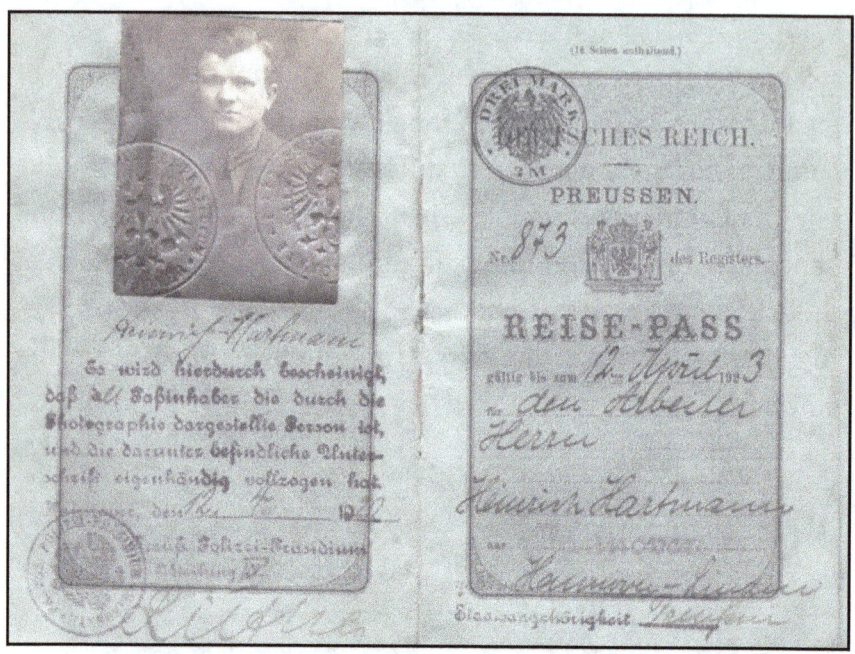

Heinrich Hartmann—My grandfather's passport from Germany to the United States. My dad had this and it is the ONLY photo I have of my grandfather under the age of 60.

RELIGIOUS AND FAITH-BASED DOCUMENTS

From baptisms, first communions, confirmations, giving records and more, any of these help us understand, remember and, perhaps, continue to celebrate traditions of faith.

I'm betting you come across interesting finds in your old inherited photo collections. It's vital to find these and connect them to the photos you may have so that these stories are preserved. Care should be taken to not inadvertently or carelessly throw these away in the future.

A client's father's Holy Communion Certificate from 1902.

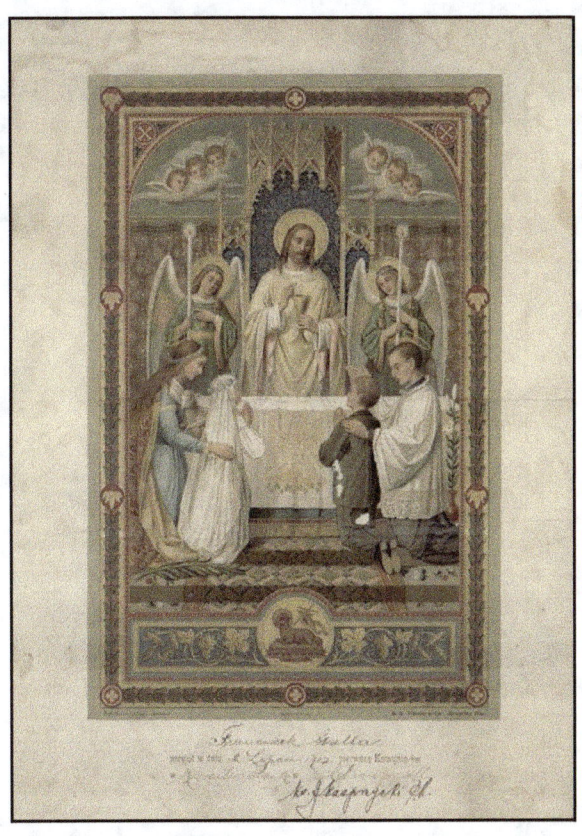

That wraps up our quick primer on the types of photos and documents you could find while organizing old albums and boxes of family photos.

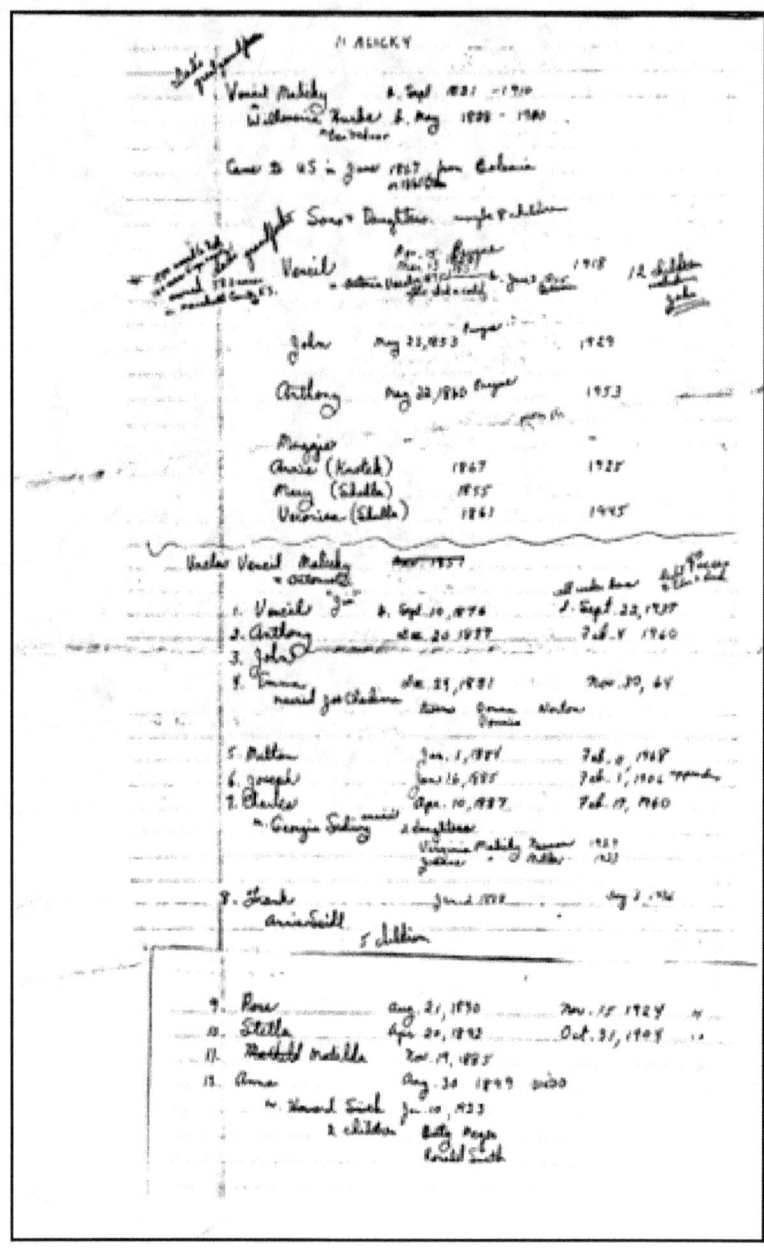

A handwritten family tree found in the bins of family photos

CHAPTER 4

ORGANIZING THE OLD PHOTOS AND DOCUMENTS

s it really necessary to organize the photos? Why not quickly go through everything and pull out the interesting stuff?

Sure, you could start selecting old photos from a variety of places and worry about organizing the rest of the mess later. Many people have done it that way, thinking there would be more time another day. But I promise you, that day will never come. Consider the following situations we have encountered:

- A family donates an old World War II scrapbook of photos because nobody wants it
- The person who inherits those old boxes of photos decides there's no value and tosses the whole mess
- Another family unknowingly donates old bins of photos and historical documents to a local thrift store
- Film reels are tossed because the projector is broken; thinking that nothing worthwhile would be on the film

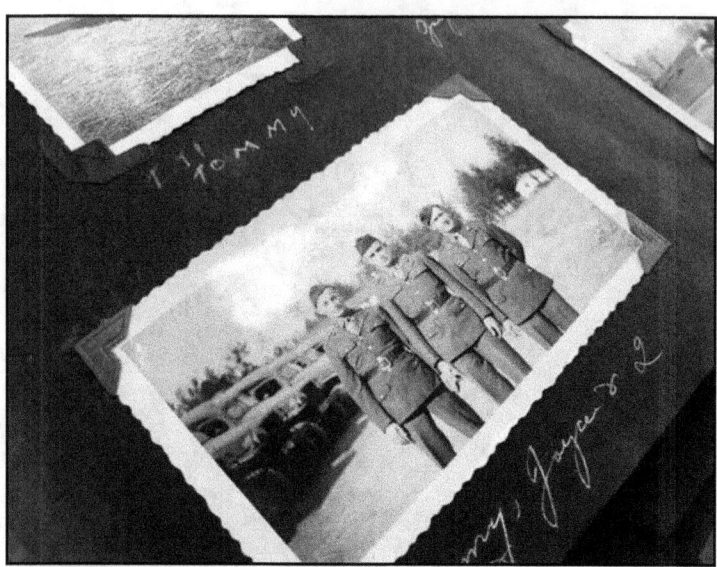

Page from a military scrapbook. Those men served our country and the entire scrapbook was donated to a military museum.

You've held on to those boxes for a reason. It's time to organize your photos once and for all, so that your children or the next generations of your family don't have to decide what to do with the old boxes of photos. And, they are much less likely to WANT to inherit all of that.

In this chapter, I share our system of organizing photos to help you get through it all as efficiently as possible. We organize photos in stages, so that no single part overwhelms us. Before getting to that, let's talk about what tools you need to organize photos.

TOOLS FOR PHOTO ORGANIZATION

Over the years, we have compiled a list of tools and tricks of the trade for working with old photos. Here's a potential list of supplies you'll need to get through the photo organizing work:

- A clipboard to hold your most important notes and information to track your project

- A variety of containers that can hold photos

- Index cards and sticky notes – for dividing batches or sections of photos

- Photo labeling pencil – to write on the back of photos notes if desired

- Spatula – to help remove photos from stick albums. If the photos are particularly stuck, sometimes dental floss can help get under the photo as needed. If the photo will be damaged, then leave it in for flatbed scanning.

- Gloves – if you have fragile or brittle photos, these can help protect the photo from the oils on your fingers. Also, gloves protect you from mold if the photos have been stored in damp places.

- Blue tape – An option to use on your table to divide up areas for sorting photos. If you can leave the tape in place, this is helpful to write the name of your sorting categories on the tape.

- Age chart – Determine the ages of the people for whom you are sorting photos, create an age chart to know how old they were in each year. Use the QR code to download an Age Chart template.

Age Chart QR code

- Archival photo boxes for when you have finished
- Sketch paper to draw out family tree – various markers, highlighters and pens

START SKETCHING OUT YOUR FAMILY TREE

With my clients' photo organizing projects, I sketch out the family tree as I go along. Generally, I'll have the immediate family information to start. As clues become available in the sorting process, I add to the sketch.

I leave creating an official family tree as a second phase of the project. So, during the photo organizing phase, I don't spend time going to a computer program or Ancestry.com to fill in a digital family tree yet. This would be a rabbit hole of distraction and we need to be efficient to get the photo organizing done!

On the opposite page is a photo showing the notes jotted down while we did our best to capture one family tree. As we learned more about the client's family during the photo organizing process, we added that information on the scratch sheet of paper. Later on, of course, you can use software to create the family tree. If you have already been investigating your family's history, you may have this part done!

Okay, let's start organizing!

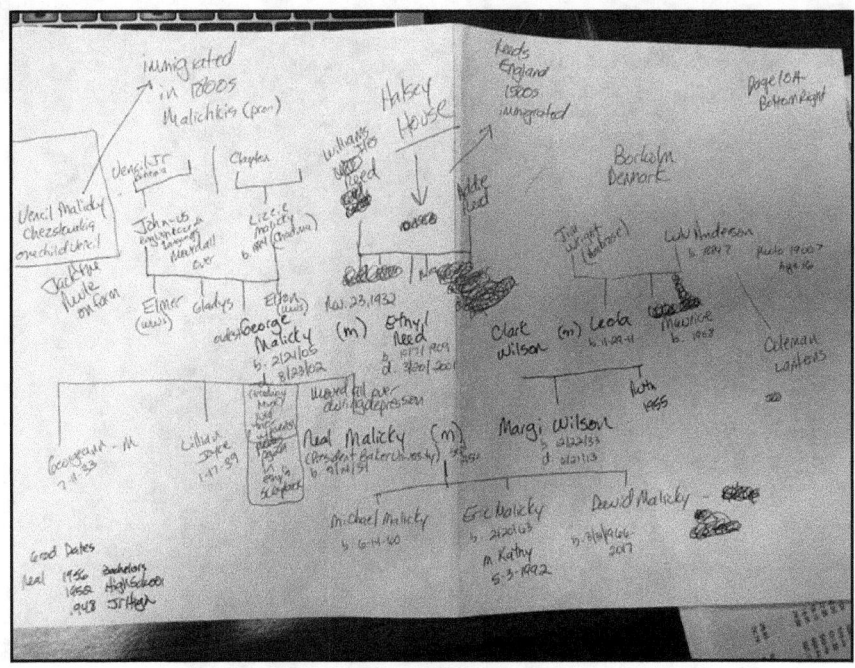

All these notes came from clues in the family photo collection.
It's not pretty, but it did the trick!

Pixologie has a full video program available on YouTube describing how a family can create its own Photo Estate. Ann and I produced these while the 2020 Covid shutdown was going on. Many people worked on their family photo projects during that unprecedented time in history.

Use this QR code to access this series on our YouTube channel.

Photo Estate Playlist QR code

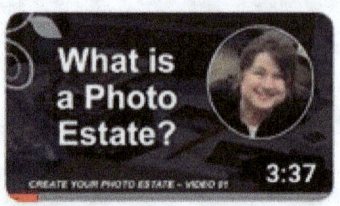

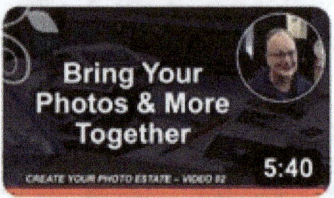

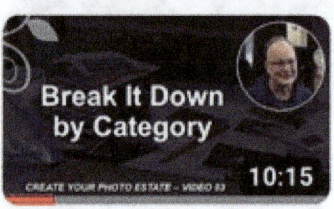

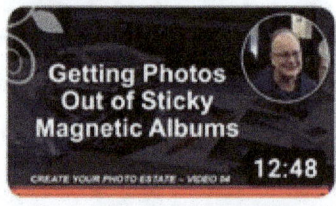

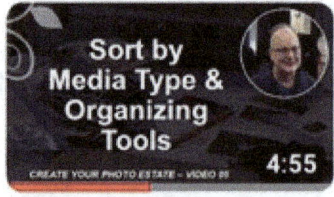

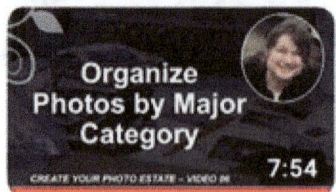

GATHER IT ALL IN ONE PLACE

We recommend finding everything from photos to memorabilia to other types of media: gathering it all to one area. This can be a large table, room or I've seen people use a bed to start stacking it all together.

I feel like this is one of the most important stages of a family photo project because it:

- Gives the project more importance and finality when it is done
- Allows for matching up duplicate, repetitive photos
- Brings batches of photos back together
- Shows us that our family members sometimes were just as disorganized as we are today with out photos!

You may be surprised to hear this, but duplicate photos were common in the 1910s, 1920s, 30s and 40s. Families shared those photos just like we did in the 1980s and 1990s. They also scrapbooked their photos and stored them in a variety of places, just like today!

In fact, I have noticed that scrapbooks from the first half of the 1900s may not have a particular order in the photographs nor a particular theme to the photos contained within.

For instance, we worked with a woman who had a scrapbook her father made after World War II. He served in Japan and actually had metal taken from a downed Japanese airplane forged into the covers of the scrapbook. While the scrapbook did contain photos of his time in the service, it also included photos of his childhood, photos from friends who married after the war, and other family photos. There was no particular order, there were duplicate photos, and similar photos that were probably not necessary to save.

As you prepare to start sorting all of your photos, be sure to gather them from all the places in the house. If you have older relatives, check with them on what photos they might have. They may even be willing to help you identify who's in the photos once you have them culled down to a manageable number. When clients bring their photo organization projects to us, we strongly encourage them to bring everything possible before we start work.

It's fun to organize and see the photos come together with our system. This is especially evident when you work with portraits. When looking at all the family portraits in one place, you can choose the portrait in the best condition, match up portrait sessions, and find important dates noted on them.

Below are thumbnail views of our client Gen's portraits as she was growing up. You can see the different portraits we

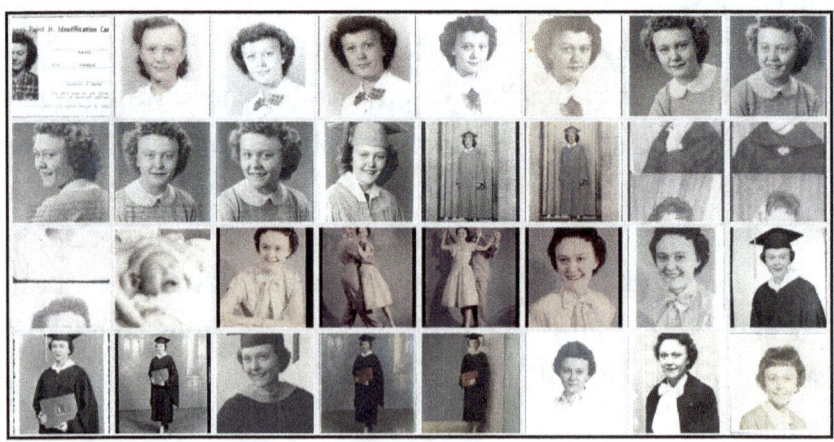

kept based on the coloring and condition of the photos. These were scattered among dozens of boxes, albums, bags, and other hiding places before we organized them.

Some people scan historical photos for different projects. A few years later, those same photos are needed again but can't be found on the computer. The originals are scanned again ... all of which leads to a digital mess. *The Pixologie system means organize once, digitize once, and preserve the images through photo books, proper back-up, and more.*

Here are some examples of bringing it all together before starting the sorting process. Clients gathered all the boxes and bins of photos they could find to bring in for organizing.

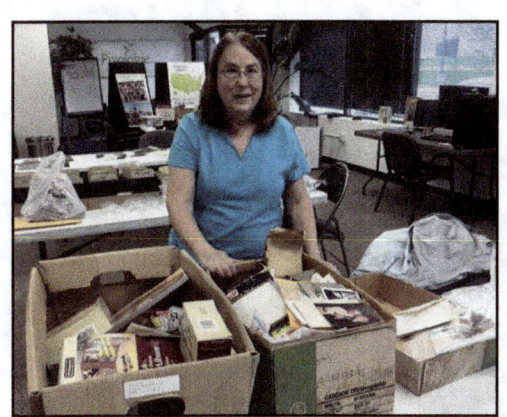
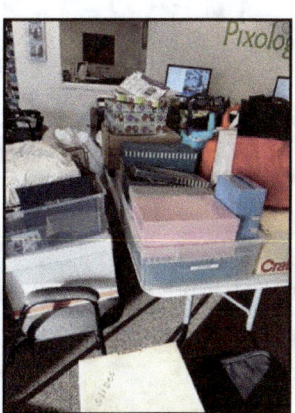

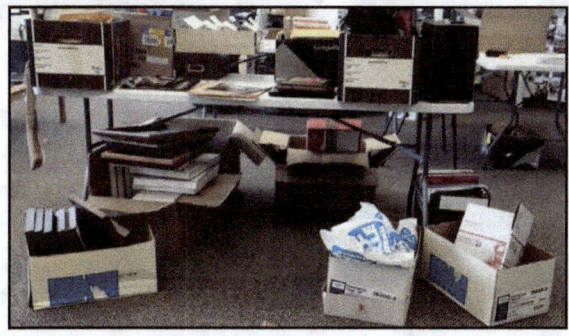

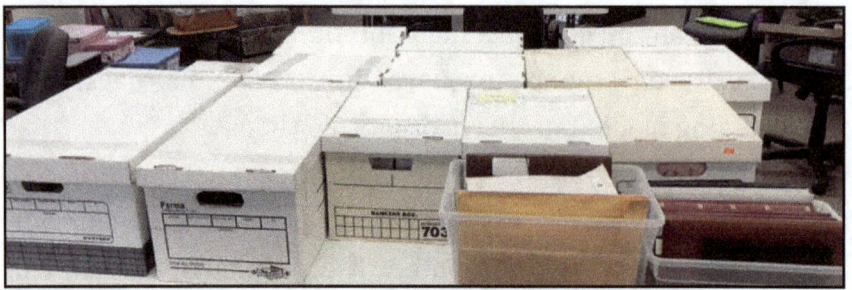

Another client has been bringing in separate projects of his parents' and grandparents' photos to scan, including:

- Two scrapbooks from the 1950s
- Loose batches of photos from his dad's childhood in the 1940s
- Negatives of his parents' wedding
- Another scrapbook of his grandfather's early adulthood
- Other loose negatives

There are similar and actual duplicate photos and groupings of photos in each batch that, in my mind, naturally belong together and should be consolidated. As we've spoken over the last year, he's realizing that he will have a challenge in working with the photos on his computer and combining the digital photos.

At the end of the day, it's better to ensure your photos are scanned even if they are not in perfect order. Scan the photos in sensible batches and then do further sorting into folders on your computer at a later time.

.

STEPS TO ORGANIZING YOUR PHOTOS

When you are ready to organize your photos, you can follow Pixologie's four steps in our general photo organizing system.

1) Sort everything by family group

2) Sort by decade

3) Break down each decade and sort by year

      A) OPTIONAL – Set aside the modern-era photos (1960s and later) to focus on the heritage photos.

4) Fine-tune each year by sorting photos by month or event.

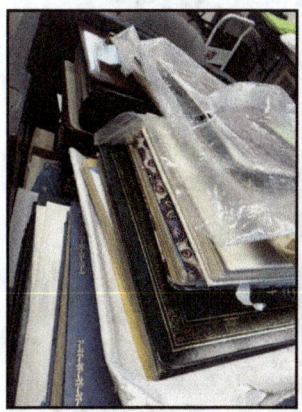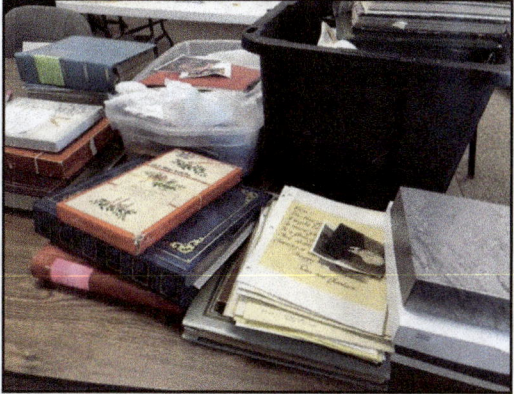

Here's a project that started off with just heaps of old family photos in two very large, very heavy-duty bins. We emptied one out on the table and you can see what was left in the other bin in the second photo.

STEP ONE - SORT BY FAMILY GROUP

If you are dealing with multiple family groups, you'll want to separate them as much as is possible without spending much time on this step at all. If you have unknown photos, you can have a bin marked "unknown" or "to sort later."

Here's is the collection of photos after sorting by family group. There was too much to start sorting by decade right away. This initial sort took just an hour or so.

In the first run-through sort of your photo collection, remember—no reminiscing, no stopping to call your sister about this fantastic photo you found. Set it all aside and focus. Your job is to go through each box, container, bin, etc. and divide out groupings (albums, boxes, bins, slides, etc) of photos by family group.

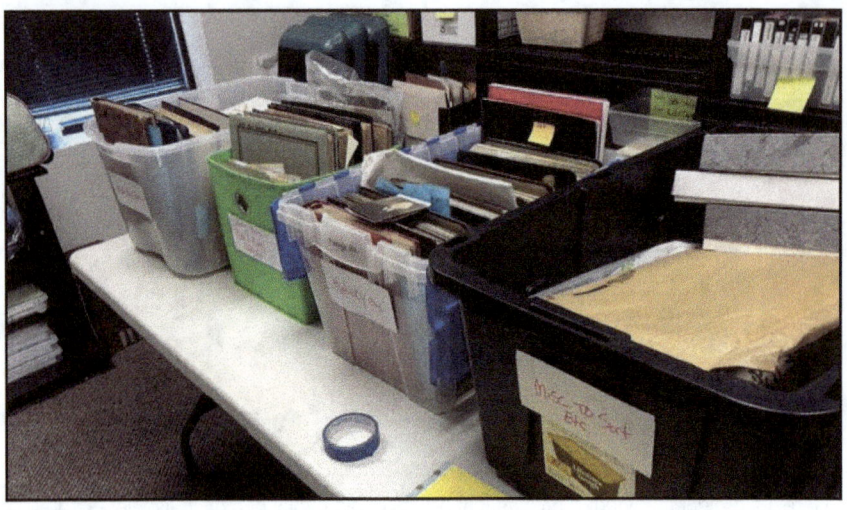

Initial sort. Each bin represents a family group

STEP TWO: SORT BY DECADE

Next up, each family group is broken down by decade. You'll want to have a box or bin for each decade. Be sure to grab your clipboard and paper to jot down notes related to your family tree.

If you don't have any idea of what decade a photo might be from; put it into an unknown bin. Have bins for memorabilia, important documents, certificates, and portraits. Here's a photo of another set of containers I used for a smaller sorting project.

I like to have a separate bin for portraits, especially the family and school portraits, because often they are more difficult to put in chronological order unless they have a date written on them. In addition, there are often so many duplicates, it really helps to have them in one place. You could have a bin for "Vintage Portraits" and for "Modern Portraits" to help divide these up in the first go round.

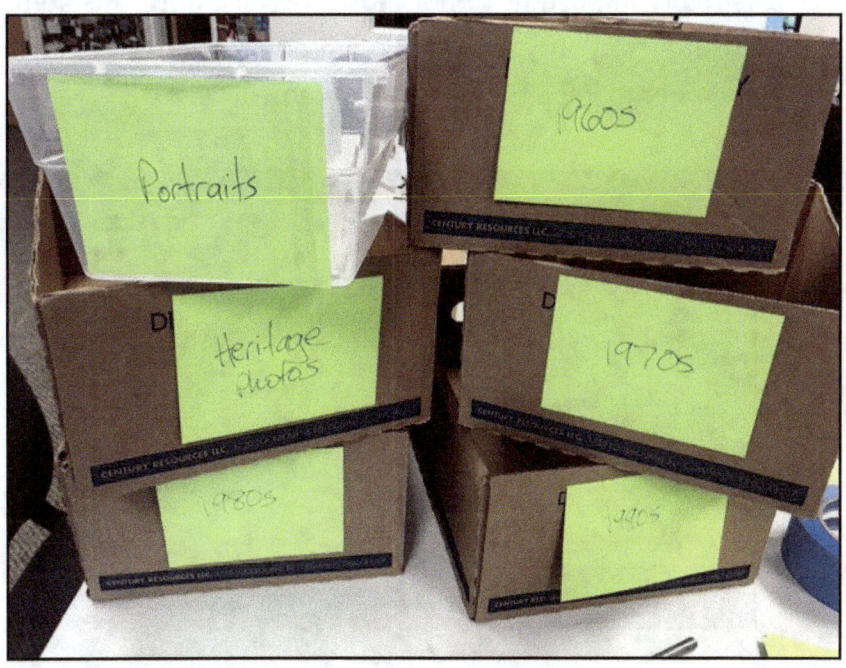

Bins for sorting by decade and type

Remember, the point is to move swiftly, not agonize over details.

If there are photos in an album or envelope, put the album or envelope in the decade bin and move on.

Right now, we just want to get through everything enough to divide it up by major family groups and decade categories. Go through all of the bins until everything is separated by decades.

In the photo below, you can see the bins we've set up and labeled. We are still working our way through the bins and boxes under the table. You also can see boxes of slides stacked up on the left-hand side. We also made sections labeled "Babies" and "Memorabilia."

It is really important to not move forward until this step is done completely. If you do have unknown photos, albums, etc., remember to keep them in an "Unknown" bin.

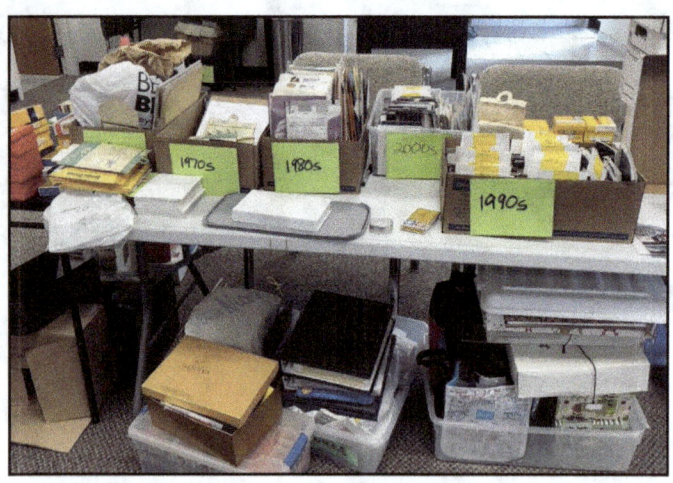

Here is a smaller project with more modern photos than old vintage ones. You can see the green divider cards listing the decade.

STEP THREE: SORT BY YEAR

Now, you will be taking each decade and start breaking it down into years. This is the time to remove photos from albums and envelopes. Use sticky notes and index cards as dividers, especially to mark timeframes.

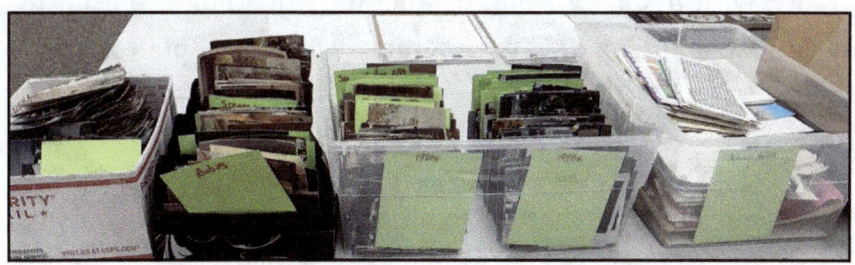

Remember, if the photo has nothing important to tell, toss it. Photos in this "toss" category include:

- Landscape scenes
- Repetitive photos of the same event
- Photos of animals (if it's from the family farm, definitely save the better photos; a handful of photos of a beloved pet, maybe)

In this stage, you are quickly looking for clues about what year the photo was taken. Clues might be as easy as a date written on the back of the photo or an envelope containing a postmark date when the photos were sent back from developing. Context clues include:

- Significant dates such as graduations, weddings, births, birthdays, etc.
- Number of children in the photos

- Fashion styles
- Date ranges written on the photo albums

We recommend working with your age chart as you do this. Work with a stack of photos and start dividing them up by year. Use an index card to separate each year of photos. More tips:

DO:
- Remove photos that are duplicates as you go
- Take photos gently out of albums (see "Tools" for more help on this)

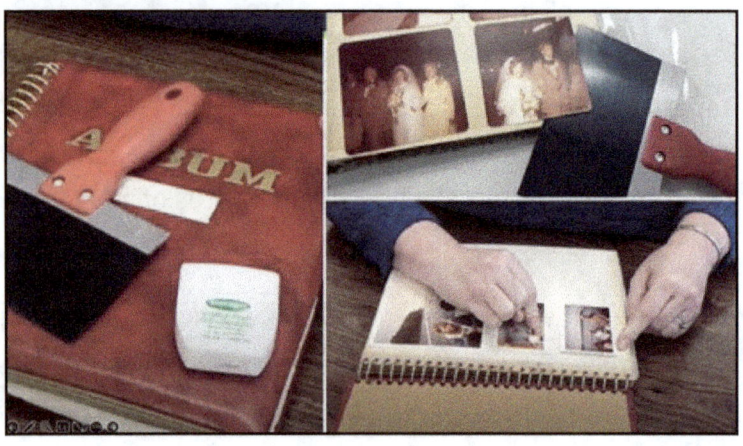

DON'T:

- Spend time trying to match photos up with other similar photos you think you've seen already.

- Worry if you can't put a year to a photo. Just stack it in the unknown pile.

It's important to just get through this step as quickly as possible. The more you linger upon it, the greater the likelihood that you will not finish the organization.

Here are photos after completing the breakdown by years for a few of our clients. In this first photo, we've organized by year. Some photo albums were left intact in keeping with our client's wishes.

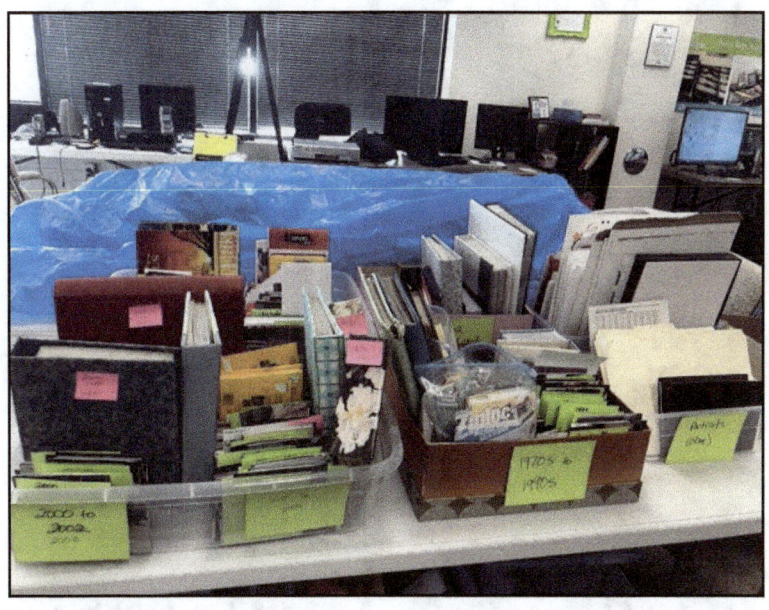

Here's an example of dating portraits. Our client Eric's maternal grandmother was Ethel Reed. Here are two family portraits. We know that Ethel was born in 1909. The first portrait, Ethel wasn't born yet but it includes all of her siblings and her parents, W.I. and Annie Reed. Fortunately, Eric's family had already identified who was who. In the second portrait, you can see many years have gone by. The children are much older and Ethel is in the back row, last on the right side. And, W.I. and Annie have aged considerably. How fascinating to see the difference. Neither photo has dates, but we can estimate the second photo may be around 1920 or later, before people started smiling in portraits.

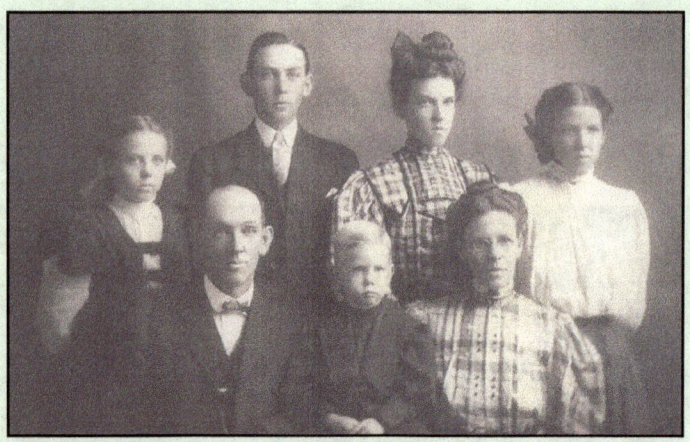

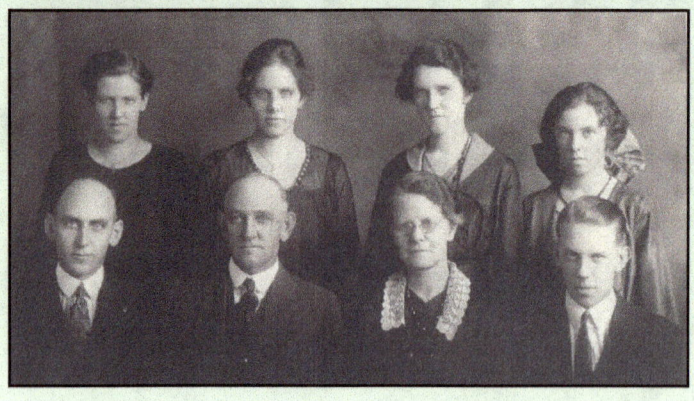

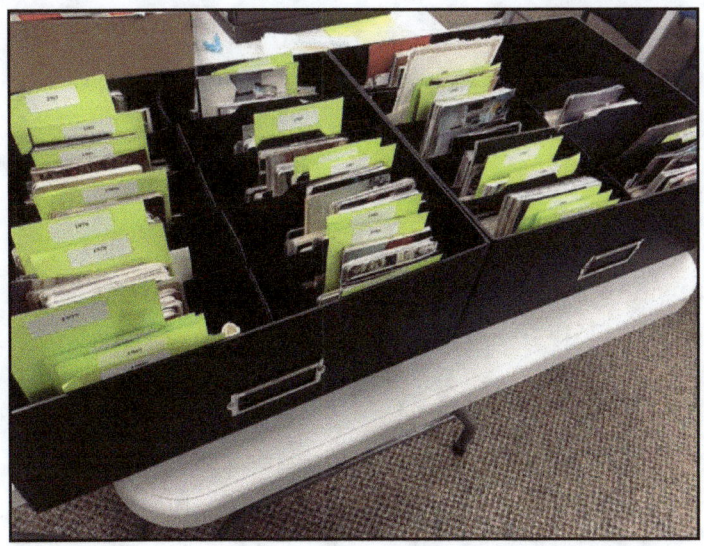

In this photo you can see, we've moved the photos to archival boxes.

STEP FOUR - FINE-TUNE THE ORGANIZATION

Once you have finished going through all of the decades and you have them separated into years, go through each year again to "fine-tune" the organization. I consider this the "curation" portion of working with your family photos. Organizing is one activity, curating takes organizing to the next level. You are preparing your collection to be viewed in the future. The work here includes choosing the best photos to save and letting others go.

During this stage, you'll be able to see groupings of photos come together, if you haven't already.

Here are some tips to curating your photos:

- Organize the years by months and/or events
- Bring groupings back together
- Remove repetitive photos
- Consider letting go unidentifiable landscape scenes with nobody in them

EXAMPLE:

Look at the screenshot below. These are 28 out of 300 scanned photos from an old, black, vintage black scrapbook of my grandmother's. She traveled with her friends and was a career woman, working as a nurses' assistant until she married. In the screenshot, you can see there are repetitive photos of the Lincoln Birthplace, landscape scenes with nobody in them and more.

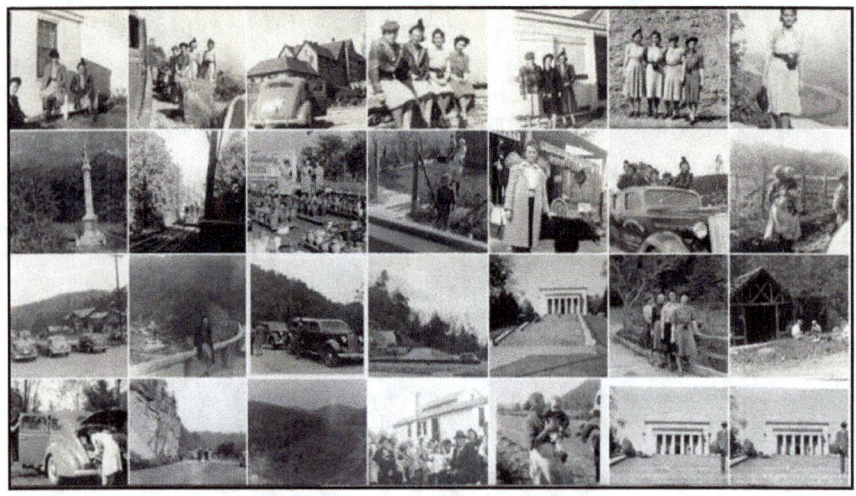

These could easily be curated down to about a dozen photos that would tell the story of an independent woman who loved roadtrips around the country in the 1940s.

In fact, you could hone it down to just one photo that captures the essence of it all. I would choose this photo:

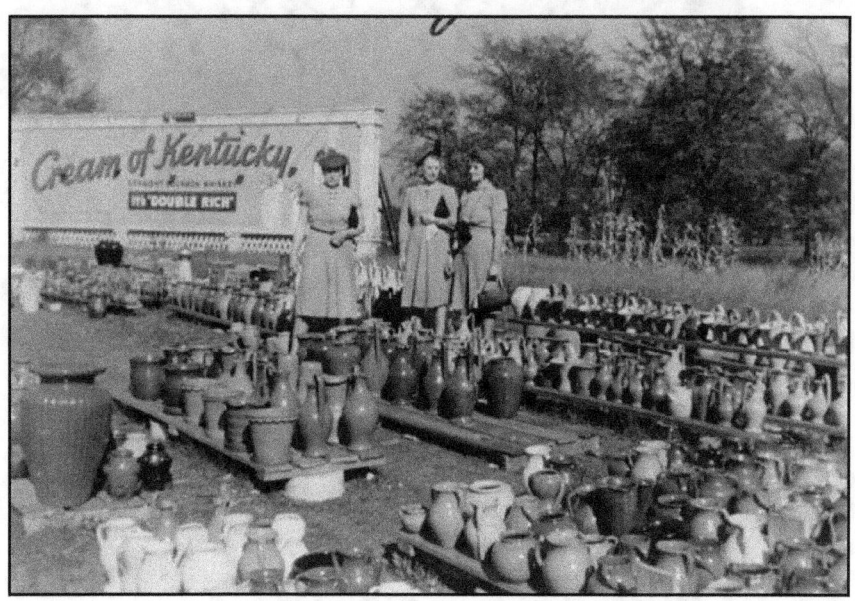

She's somewhere possibly in Kentucky at a roadside pottery stand shopping with her lady friends. It's a perfect photo to capture what my grandmother's life was like before she married and had children.

Continue to make notes on your family tree sketch as you come across pertinent family information. As you fine-tune the batches, keep in mind that each batch will be scanned into its own folder.

Once you get through the photos, work on the memorabilia bin. You can sort the certificates, letters, newspaper articles, cards, and more into meaningful stacks. You'll find duplicates of some of these items and you can keep the best copies. These will all need to be scanned as well.

EXAMPLES:

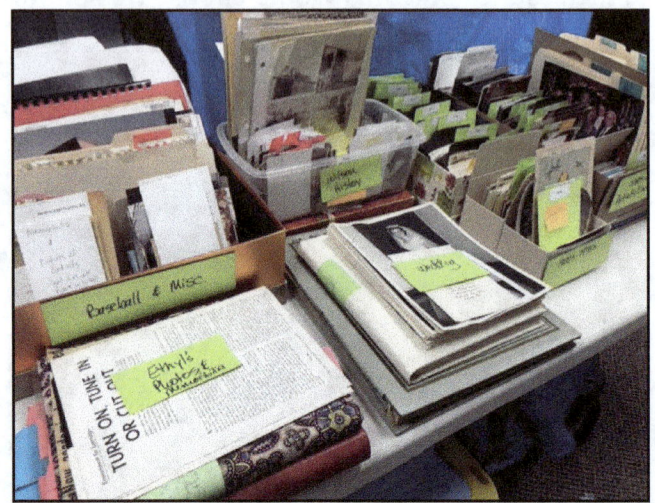

Family photos organized in batches to be scanned.

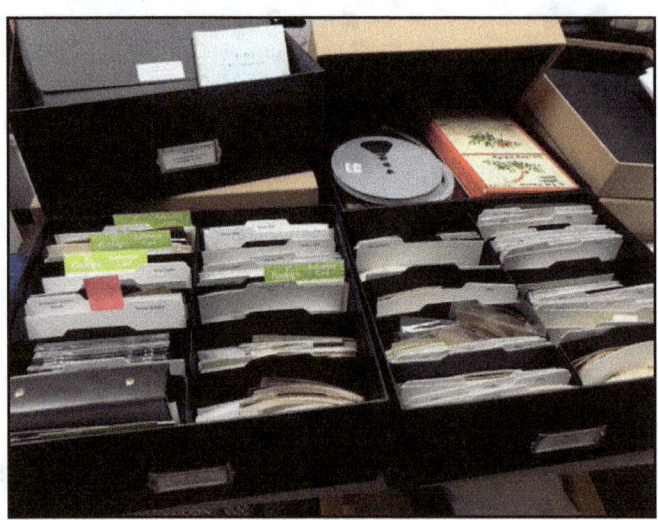

Same project now moved into archival photo boxes and labeled neatly.

In the next photo, Gen's family photo collection is in archival boxes and labeled. The tall boxes contain the over-sized portraits, certificates, letters, mortgage deeds, and more.

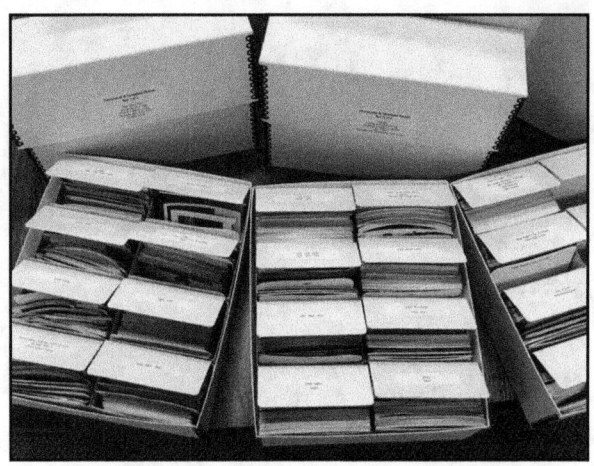

These boxes are from Archival Methods
(www.archivalmethods.com)

Let's move on to digitizing all of these family treasures. Each of the batches of photos you so carefully organized and curated will now be scanned and saved in digital folders that match the organization you just completed.

CHAPTER 5
SCAN THE OLD PHOTOS

O nce you have your photos organized, digitizing is the next step. This chapter really gets into the technical details of making sure that your digital image will be created correctly the first time. You want these photos to have a preservation-quality size and scan. If you find some of this work overwhelming or simply not something you wish to do, now might be the time to hire a professional.

Before I explain scanning options, it's important to make sure you understand file formats and dpi (dots per inch). When you scan a photo, you want to do it the right way.

FILE FORMATS
Your scanner may give you the following formats for saving a photo:

♦ **JPG or JPEG** – Named for the Joint Photographers Expert Group back in the early 1990s, the committee that created the JPG format. The JPG is today's standard digital photo format. Most cameras and smartphones save photos in the JPG format. JPG files are compressed so that the file sizes are not huge.

- ◆ Some scanners allow you to adjust the level of compression so you can determine an acceptable image quality and storage size.

- ◆ For most users, simply follow the factory settings for JPG file size and compression if there is an option

- ◆ Multiple edits to a JPG can result in significantly reduced quality of the original photo.

- ◆ We recommend scanning as JPGs for most people. However, if you plan on heavy editing and multiple versions, consider scanning as a TIFF.

- TIFF – Named Tagged Image File Format, created by Aldus Corporation for desktop publishers. They created the format back in the mid 1980s to help scanner vendors agree upon a common scanned image format. This file format is not compressed, so file sizes are very large.

  - ◆ You can edit a TIFF, save it and still have the same image quality achieved at first scanning.

  - ◆ We generally see professional photographers, graphic artists, and other similar professionals using this file format.

  - ◆ File sizes are so large (30 to 100 MB) that working with them can be very slow.

- **PDF** – Named Portable Document Format, created by Adobe in the 1990s so that business, as well as consumers, could present documents independent of software. We never scan photos as PDFs for obvious reasons. We do scan family history typed documents as PDFs because it is easier to read a PDF version than scroll through 20+ pages of family documentation scanned as photos.

If you're wondering whether to scan something as a PDF or JPG, here are some tips:

- One-page documents – Scan as a PDF or JPG. Scan as a JPG if you plan on putting it into a book, Word document, or photo book.
- More than one-page documents – Scan as a PDF for easy downloading, sharing, and printing. Only scan as individual JPGS if you need them as graphics for a book or photo book.

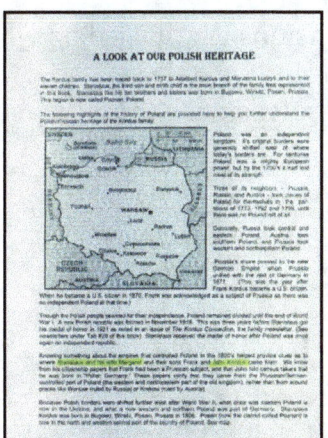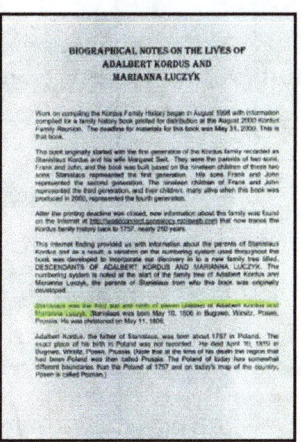

Two pages of a 20+ page family historical document.
This is better scanned as a PDF so that it is easily shared and printed.

Scanning as a PDF makes it possible to do optical character recognition (OCR), which allows for searching within the document by keywords and for copying or editing of the document. This is extremely beneficial for archiving and sharing genealogical information. A great example is for the scanning of a church record. If you scan as a JPG, it's easy to look at but if you scan it as a PDF and then apply OCR, you can search for names and more.

- PNG – Portable Network Graphic – This file format allows easy digital sharing with small file sizes. You create a PNG when you take a screenshot of something on your computer, tablet, or smartphone.

- HEIF – High Efficiency Image Format. With use beginning in 2013, Apple adopted the HEIF format for iPhone users in 2017. This format contains the same high-quality image as a JPG but uses somewhere around half of the storage space. If you have HEIF images, you may need to convert them to JPGs or TIFFs.

- Camera Raw Formats – Extensions vary based on what camera you are using. Generally, we only see these formats with hobbyist and professional photographers.

DPI - WHAT RESOLUTION TO USE?

Most scanners allow you to change the scanning resolution setting or the DPI setting. DPI stands for dots per inch and the higher the DPI, the more detail is caught as you scan the image.

Scanning DPI generally can range from 72 DPI up to 1200 DPI. As you can imagine, the higher the DPI, the larger the digital file size. For photo scanning, we choose scanning settings for family archive projects to be either at 600 DPI or 1200 DPI.

We generally recommend scanning photos at 600 DPI and tiny (less than 1 x 2) photos at 1200 DPI.

For restoration purposes, if you scan at 1200 DPI, it is more difficult to restore a photo as the scanner captures the grain of the paper. This can make it harder for the restorer to improve the damaged image.

As long as you remember to change the DPI setting to at least 600 DPI, you can feel good about the size of scan. Some scanners have additional settings to create and/or adjust high quality JPGs which may allow for less compression of the digital photo. Again, you can increase the quality settings, but remember, the file size will go up as well.

* * *

Okay, now that we have covered file formats and resolution, let's talk about some of the scanning options available.

Scanning Options

Depending upon the number of photos you have to scan, you'll want to think about which option may be right for you. Also, are many of your photos fragile or stuck to album pages?

Your Printer/Scanner - Yes, you can scan photos with your printer/scanner in a pinch if you need. Using your printer to scan a large number of photos takes a very long time. Typically, your printer/scanner comes with software that allows you to save your scans in a folder on your computer.

Here's a screenshot of the software on my Mac that I use to scan photos and documents. When I opened it, the resolution was set to 75 dpi and format was set to JPEG. 75 DPI looks great on a screen but doesn't produce a printable image. You can also see the words "Scan To," which allows you to locate exactly where on your computer to save the scans. I don't have the option of naming the images. However, I can place several pictures on the scanner and Auto Selection will detect and save separate items.

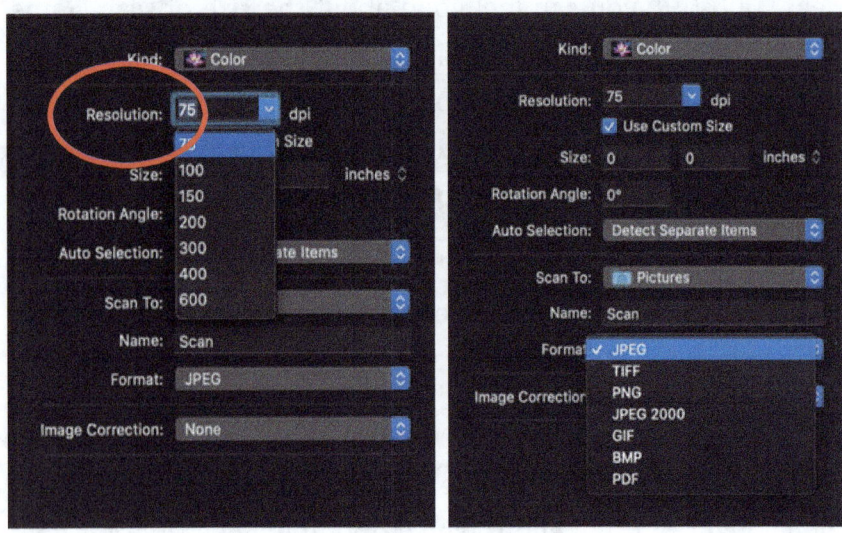

Printer/scanner optional settings

The Epson FastFoto FF-680W Wireless High-speed Photo and Document Scanning System – Priced around $600, this consumer-grade scanner has been earning high reviews all the way around.

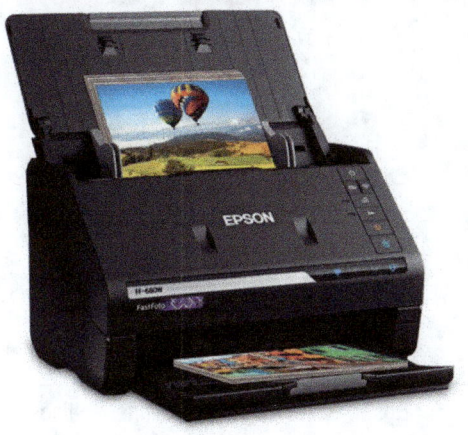

This Epson can scan one photo a second at 300 DPI. At 600 DPI, it still scans your photos fast. For fragile photos and documents, Epson offers carrier sheets to send the photos through the scanner.

You do need to clean the scanner often as it picks up dust easily. The scanner will occasionally remind you to check for streaks as well.

We use this scanner at Pixologie, especially for photos from the 1960s and 1970s, with the "color restore" on (located in the Scanner Settings).

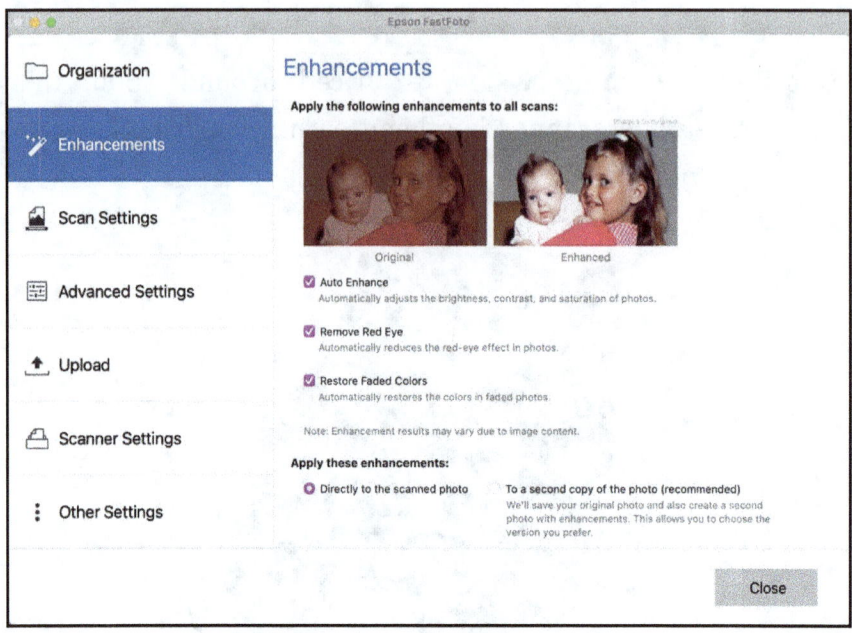

Epson Fast Foto 680W scanner settings.

Just a quick note about Color Restore and Photo Enhancement. In general, we turn these options off preferring to save the original photo as scanned with the exception of the 1960s and 1970s photos. Then, we use our own software to adjust color, brightness, sharpness etc.

This may be a good idea if you are going to want to do your own editing of the photo in the future. By saving the original photo, you'll be starting from scratch. If you save both the original and the scanner's edited version (the Epson Fastfoto 680 offers this), now you may end up with two photos to save. If you only save the scanner's edited version, then you may in the future be editing an already edited version of your photo.

Food for thought!

In the end, future generations will be happy to have either versions or both of the photos if the pictures are saved neatly in digital folders or albums.

Many other Flatbed Photo Scanner **options** – Epson and other companies make a variety of flatbed scanners that are considerably less expensive than a high-speed scanner.

Some of these flatbed scanners come with a dual light source, which allows you to scan negatives and slides as well. I always go to Best Buy and Amazon to read consumer reviews before I order a new scanner. Here's a popular choice:

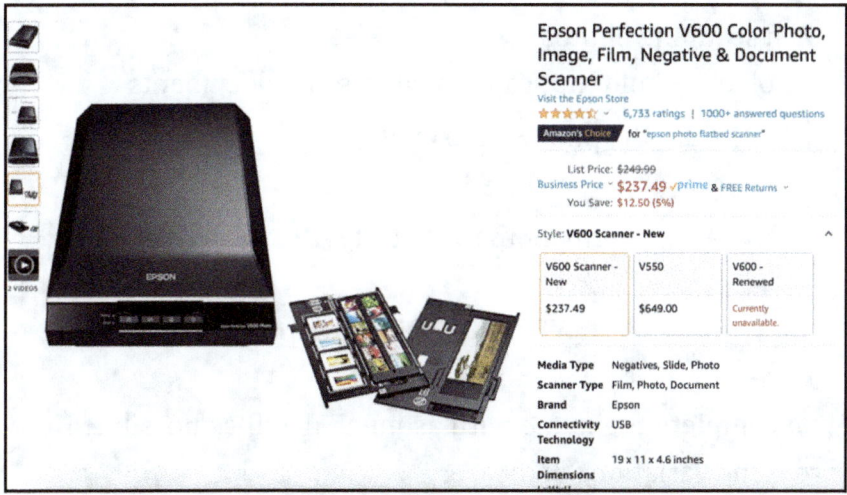

The Epson V600 has over 6,700 reviews and an overall 4.5 star rating.

TAKING PHOTOS OF OLD PICTURES

In general, we don't recommend taking pictures of old family photos, especially with a cell phone. I do know that there are professionals out there who are "camera scanning" and have studios set up to take high-quality photos of images. We have not employed that method at Pixologie. We feel that direct scanning typically keeps you closer to the original image.

In some cases, with very large portraits or convex bubble glass portraits, using a scanner is not an option. Then, we do use a professional-grade camera to photograph the portraits.

NAMING CONVENTIONS FOR YOUR SCANNED PHOTOS

"How should I name my ancestor's photos and documents?" When I give presentations on photo organization, I hear this question a lot.

Keep in mind there are two items we are working with when scanning photos.

- Folders – hold the scanned photos and documents
- Files – are the photos, documents, etc.

When working with photos, we start with the folders:

YYYY-MM-DD Description

You complete the name with as much detail as possible. Here are some variations of its use:

- 1900s-1930s Photos
- 1955-12-08 Stanley and Helen Kordus Wedding
- 1976 Family Photos

By naming folders this way, they will be organized in chronological order.

Then, we make sure the digital photo files are named the same as the folder. This eliminates making another decision about naming which can slow you down.

Epson scanners allow you to choose your folder and name your photos. We set up our Epson scanners to name the photos with the YYYY-MM-DD Description format.

YYYY-MM-DD Description_00001.jpg

Examples include:

- 1920s Photos_00001.jpg
- 1920s Photos_00002.jpg
- 1964 Photos_00001.jpg
- 1985-12 Christmas_00001.jpg

If you have to rename them, you'll want to use a program that allows you to use a three-, four- or five-digit counter. (i.e. 001, 0001 or 00001; the examples above have a five-digit counter.)

Adobe Bridge and XNViewMP are two programs we use to rename photos.

Simply take a photo of the QR code to go to the YouTube video that shows how to use XNView MP to rename your photo.

Use XNView MP to rename photos

Be careful renaming scans in Windows File Explorer. There is no option to use a counter and instead you end up with something that looks like this:

1980s Hartmann Children (1)	12/1/2019 10:04 AM	JPG File	780 KB
1980s Hartmann Children (2)	12/1/2019 10:04 AM	JPG File	697 KB
1980s Hartmann Children (3)	12/1/2019 10:04 AM	JPG File	709 KB
1980s Hartmann Children (4)	12/1/2019 10:04 AM	JPG File	856 KB
1980s Hartmann Children (5)	12/1/2019 10:04 AM	JPG File	540 KB
1980s Hartmann Children (6)	12/1/2019 10:04 AM	JPG File	714 KB
1980s Hartmann Children (7)	12/1/2019 10:04 AM	JPG File	686 KB
1980s Hartmann Children (8)	12/1/2019 10:04 AM	JPG File	557 KB
1980s Hartmann Children (9)	12/1/2019 10:04 AM	JPG File	599 KB
1980s Hartmann Children (10)	12/1/2019 10:04 AM	JPG File	720 KB
1980s Hartmann Children (11)	12/1/2019 10:04 AM	JPG File	708 KB
1980s Hartmann Children (12)	12/1/2019 10:04 AM	JPG File	803 KB

It's possible that the order can be mixed up in some situations, depending on the software you use to manage your photo collection. Some programs will place (1), (10), (11), (12) in order because it reads all of the ones coming first.

I have always thought this system of "YYYY-MM-DD Description" worked well for most photo-organizing projects. However, naming folders this way does not clearly show family lineages.

When dealing with six, seven, or more generations of historical photos and documents, I have begun using a folder numbering system that I'll talk further about in the next chapter. Here's a preview of how I name folders dealing with family ancestors:

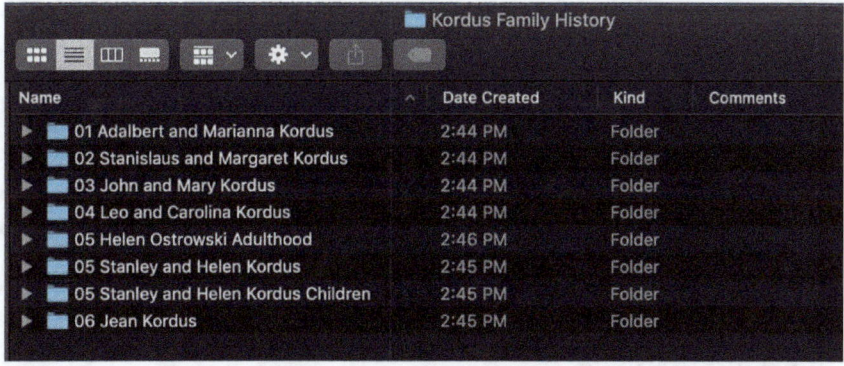

You can see I am in the Kordus Family History Folder, which contains family members numbered by generation. Adalbert and Marianna Kordus are the first generation for which I have any documents to preserve. I'll be explaining this further in the second part of this book.

You'll want to think about the naming of your folders, especially if you have several sides of family photos to scan.

Start Scanning

When you start scanning batches of photos, please be sure to check your output folders to ensure your files are being scanned and named as you expected.

As you go about scanning photos, remember to switch to new folders and naming when you start the next family batch of photos.

If you wish, you can find a local person or business to scan your photos for you. Our local camera stores scan photos. If you are sending photos out to be scanned, we recommend using very reputable, trackable shipping. Pixologie only uses Fed Ex to handle our client's treasured memories, and we would be happy to scan your photos.

Once the photos are scanned, they should now be named in a format that will help you save your family history and tell their stories. In the past, people wrote names, dates, and places on the backs of photos. Now, many people add comments and locations to the scanned photos to provide additional information.

ADDING INFORMATION TO THE DIGITAL PHOTO - METADATA

Every digital photo, whether scanned or taken with a digital camera, contains metadata. Metadata provides documentation for data products, including digital photos, documents, videos, and more. In essence, metadata answers who, what, when, where, why, and how about every facet of the data that are being documented. The International Press Telecommunications Corps (IPTC) offers a great deal of information on their website about metadata. (1)

Photo metadata:

- describes and provides information about the rights and administration of an image.
- allows information to be transported with an image file, in a way that can be understood by other software and human users.

- includes the pixels of image files are created by automated capture from cameras or scanners.

There are three types of photo metadata:

1) Descriptive (title, caption, tags)

2) Administrative (creation date, location, etc)

3) Rights (creator, copyright, credits)

After scanning, you may eventually wish to add the family information to your digital photos' metadata in the caption, title, or tags area. You do need to be careful which fields you edit. In some cases, your family will not be able to see your information, depending upon how they view the final photo.

There are many ways to add metadata. If you'd like to learn more, you can go to this video that I produced on YouTube.

Working with metadata
QR code

In addition, you may want to visit the Facebook Family History Metadata Working Group to learn more about the work other people in the field are doing to help create consistency in how metadata is handled. (2)

HIRE SOMEONE TO SCAN YOUR COLLECTION

If you would like to hire someone to scan your photos, check your local business listings. Be sure to ask them to scan and save your photos in folders labeled with the batch name. At Pixologie, we would love to help you with your scanning. Visit our website to schedule a consultation or to learn more!

It's easy to feel safe once you have scanned your old photos and other items. However, you must preserve the digital files. We'll dive into that next.

CHAPTER 6

PRESERVING OLD PHOTOS AND DOCUMENTS

P art of preserving your photo collection includes ensuring the photos and documents (print and/or digital) will be around for generations in the future. Many people have lost their digital files to unfortunate situations. A lost drive, a crashed computer, and many other reasons can lead to heartache and frustration.

We'll first talk about archival boxes for the physical photos and documents. Then, we'll discuss preserving the digital files.

ARCHIVAL BOXES

You may wish to purchase photo- and document-safe storage for your collection, either before or after you have completed your organization. We recommend waiting until step three or four, as you may have much less to save than you expected. Either way, if you wish to preserve the physical photos and documents, you'll need archival boxes.

We use products from Archival Methods and love how the boxes color coordinate and have metal reinforced corners.

Archival Methods carries polyethylene bags, sleeves, and much more to protect your photo collection.

Some families like a more decorative archival box and we offer these archival boxes, which hold up to 2,300 photos These are a true treasure to hand down to the next generation. In some cases, our clients use these boxes for their entire photo sorting process. The individual compartments and index cards are user-friendly.

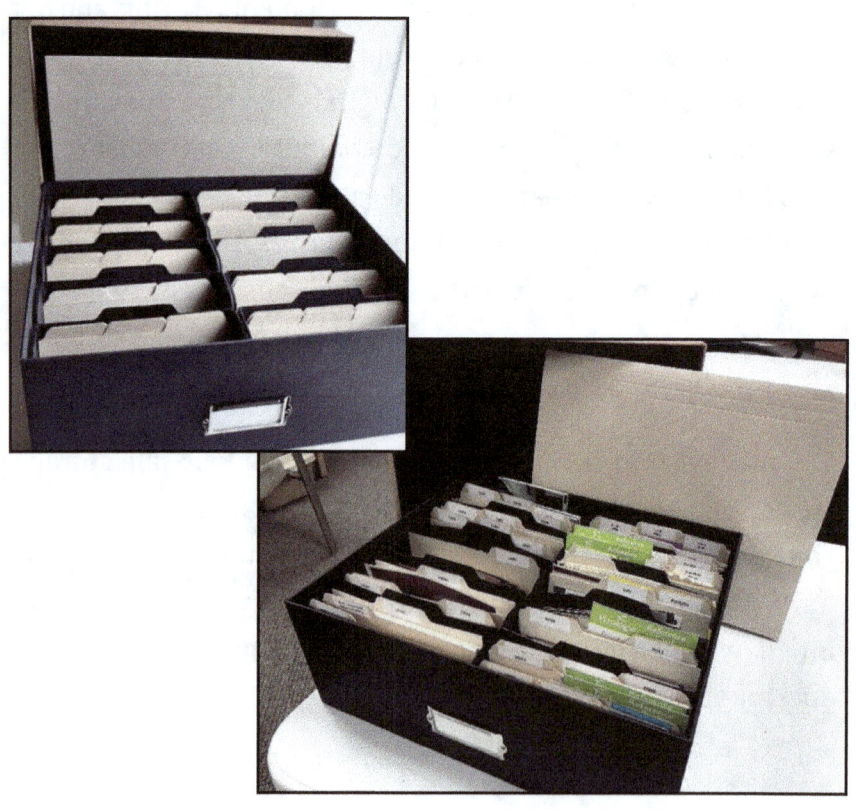

OTHER OPTIONS

There are other companies that sell archival-quality storage boxes. Look for your archiving products to be PVC-, lignin-, and acid-free.

If you are storing other fragile items with non-paper characteristics (leather, etc.), you should also explore whether products should be buffered. Buffered boxes and paper contain properties to help counteract acids that may form in the material being preserved.

Newspaper clippings and other non-photo materials should be preserved separately from photos. These materials can contain acid and can cause damage in the long term to your photos.

BOOKS & MEMOIRS

You can preserve your collection physically by creating photo books and family memoirs. Imagine in the future that one of your descendants is looking through a modern-day photo book. They will love seeing what life was like in our times and learning about the family adventures we experienced.

If ever technology were to disappear, these books and the archival boxes may be the only connection our future families have to us.

Imagine the unimaginable and our future generations only inherited the physical items we have preserved. It would be similar to our experience of inheriting old heirloom photos, fragile, dusty documents in old script, and crumbling black scrapbooks.

Photo Books

If creating a photobook or writing a family memoir seems overwhelming, you feel the same as many other people who still want to preserve their family history and photo collection. Fortunately, there are more services than ever to help with this process.

Storyworth.com – This company offers a valuable, affordable service. You purchase a one-year subscription for around $99. You are buying the subscription for someone to tell their stories. Once a week, choose a question to inspire someone to write. They'll simply reply with an email, which is shared with you. At the end of a year, their stories are bound into a beautiful keepsake book.

Biographbook.com – This is an up and coming biography service you may want to learn more about. Founder Aaron Greenberg is a fellow University of Wisconsin alumni and I enjoyed learning about the company's plans to help people preserve their stories. From their website:

> "A privacy-forward storytelling app, Biograph is a new way to create and gather memory. Think of it as a living memoir, preserving your experience in real time. Creatively tell your story. Biograph is designed for you—not advertisers. Securely record moments and transform your memory into a super-power. Record, organize, and collaborate. Snap photos and narrate stories with friends. AI transcription powers your own personal search engine. Biograph is your tool—wield it as you wish."

AUDIO STORIES

Advances in technology make it easy to record audio family histories and biographies. Here are a few options to use:

- Otter.ai – Records and transcribes conversations using the power of artificial intelligence. Your transcription most likely will need edits but it is a fantastic tool. You can get started for free to record 30 minute conversations.

- Use your phone to record conversations and interviews

- Set up your computer with a high-quality microphone to record

- Online services like "To Be Told Again"

- Hire a personal historian or biographer who may likely record conversations as well.

Whatever option you use, be sure to save your final recording in a safe place in your home as well as online. For now, let's continue with ensuring the digital items are backed up and preserved properly.

EXTERNAL HARD DRIVE BACK-UP OPTIONS

In this day and age, you'll find many options for backing up your photos, including physical back-ups as well as cloud-based back-ups. We recommend you have one back-up in the house and two outside of the house.

External Hard Drive – Both PC and Mac computers come with software to connect to an external hard drive. You can set the back-up to occur as often as you like. On a PC, you can use the FileHistory feature to back up and on a Mac, use the Time Machine to back up your computer's folders and files.

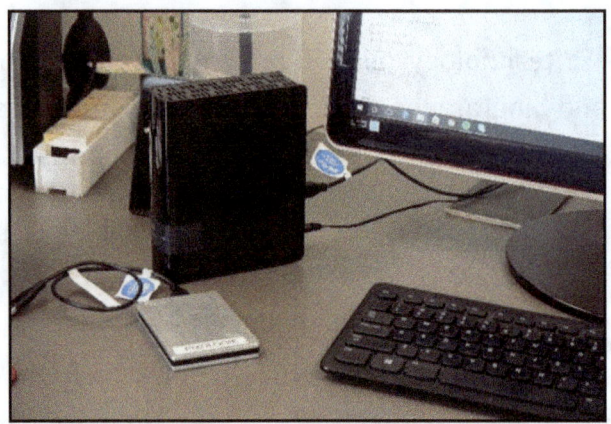

Two types of external hard drives: one small, portable one and one large desktop drive. Either one will work for your in-home back-up.

Alternatively, you can simply copy your digital photo collection to an external hard drive. However, it's very difficult to keep this up when you may be adding just a small number of photos on a routine basis to your collection.

Also, keep in mind that attached drives are susceptible to the same attacks of viruses and malware that may plague your computer. A continuously connected external hard drive cannot safely be considered a backup.

For your copies stored outside the house, you could use another external hard drive. You might put it in a safe deposit box or at a family member's home. However, it is impractical to keep running over to that location to update the external hard drive when you have new photos to add to the back-up. You may want to consider a cloud back-up service.

CLOUD-BASED BACK-UP OPTIONS

There are many cloud-based computer back-up services available including Carbonite, iDrive, and Backblaze. These services back up all your computer's files. In the event of a computer crash, you can download your folders and files or the company will send your files back for you to restore to your computer.

Cautionary note: Please do not depend upon a cloud service being your ONLY back-up. While Carbonite and Backblaze have been around a long time, many technology companies have come and gone. Also, we have heard client stories where the back-up they counted on did not work properly and important files were lost.

These computer back-up services do not allow for easy viewing and enjoyment of your collection.

OTHER ONLINE CLOUD STORAGE

The Internet offers "free" cloud storage for photos, including Google. Paid cloud storage options include Amazon and Dropbox, among many others. We caution our clients about most website photo storage for a number of reasons, including:

- Some "free" sites pay for storing your photos by selling your information or even access to your photos. If you use one of these sites, be sure to review the agreement and make sure you are not signing away the rights to your personal photos. And be aware that your personal information may be used for marketing research and other purposes.

- With the fast mergers, changes, and closures that occur in technology companies, the website may not be around in a few years. We have had clients lose access to their photos because the company closed or merged with another company and service ended for online photo storage.

- The photo storage site may not keep the highest resolution of your photo

- Photos may be difficult to download and may not retain the metadata of the photo (i.e., the comments and tags you have added, the date taken)

- After you are gone, there is no guarantee your family will have access to the photos you have preserved.

For short-term reasons, some of these websites may be beneficial to having a second back-up of your photo collection. However, you might be interested to learn of a more permanent cloud solution.

FOREVER - An Option for Future Generations

Since 2014, I have watched a company named FOREVER, Inc. develop permanent cloud photo storage from its early start-up phase through today. Founder Glen Meakem wanted a place where people could safely store all of their family photos, video, and documents. And, his vision included the passing on of this collection to future generations.

From FOREVER's website:

> "With FOREVER, you can edit, organize, store, and share your photos. Rest easy knowing your content will always be safe in your permanent digital home at FOREVER. All of this is

possible because of the FOREVER Guarantee and our easy-to-use web, mobile, and desktop apps."

I have referenced FOREVER accounts briefly in this book so far. As a "FOREVER Ambassador," Pixologie routinely recommends that people consider FOREVER, the permanent photo storage company. (Please also note that Pixologie receives a commission when people use its links to purchase FOREVER.)

You can purchase 10GB of storage for a one-time fee of $219, which can hold 2,500 to 5,000 photos. A portion of that purchase goes into the "FOREVER" Guarantee Fund, which promises to migrate your photos to the newest technology for the next 100 years.

> For a complimentary trial account, visit www.forever.com/ambassador/pixologieinc. You'll receive 2 GB of storage, enough for 200-500 photos and a $20 coupon, which can be used for any FOREVER product.

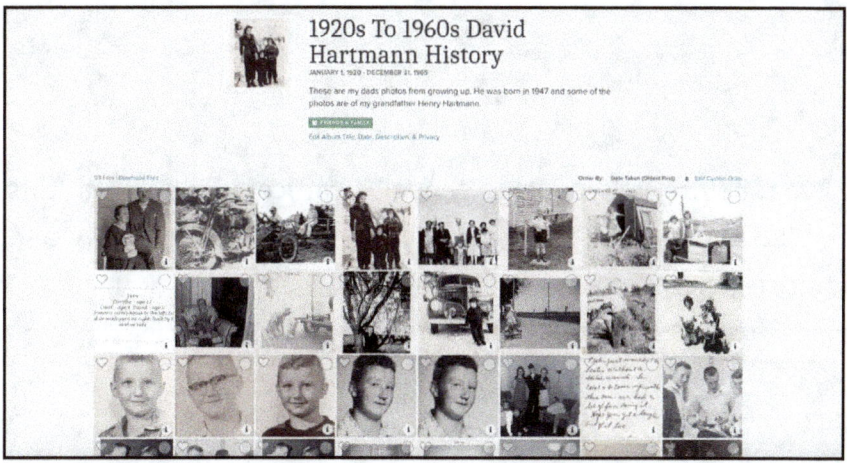

This is my FOREVER album, where I store my father's heritage photos.

Even with storing photos in FOREVER, I still recommend keeping a digital back-up in your home. FOREVER is accessed through the Internet. If you are without Internet and/or electricity, you will not have access to your FOREVER account.

Along with the ability to create photo books and gifts, as well as order prints, FOREVER now offers Family Research in its services.

* * *

This concludes the first section of the book, "Working With Your Family Photos."

You have a plan to get your old photos organized, scanned, and preserved. By completing this work, you will have created a family photo estate, which is ...

> *"...a printed or digital collection of photos, film, video, documents ,and memorabilia organized in a manner that allows another person or persons to view the photos, learn about the lives documented and be impacted by the legacy of those people."*

Even before adding the genealogical components to this collection, you are giving a gift to yourself, your family and future generations to come.

Now it's time to talk genealogy!

Section Two
Working with Your
Family Genealogy

Okay, we have covered the topic of preserving your photo collection. Let's move on to Section Two of this book, diving into preserving your family genealogy. It is truly amazing to see your photos and documents come together to tell your ancestors' stories.

CHAPTER 7

ORGANIZING YOUR GENEALOGICAL MATERIALS

As we dive into preserving your family genealogy, I want to address how Pixologie's organizational methods can complement saving corresponding genealogical documents and memorabilia.

Early on in our photo organizing work, I realized standard genealogical methods would not fit well with photos. It especially came to light when I was working with one client who had photos covering seven generations of extended family.

If you are looking to preserve your family genealogy in a standard genealogical format, there are many resources in the back of this book.

For genealogical purposes, there are several official ways to organize family members in a text format through the use of numbering. They include the:

- Ahnentafel Method
- Atree Method
- Surname Method

- Register System
- NGSQ System
- and more

All of these are more complicated than I want to ever tackle. To be honest, I researched the options and I felt overwhelmed. Using complicated number systems just doesn't work for my personal situation and for our clients at Pixologie.

As a photo organizer, I have always taught that we don't need to save every moment ever photographed. We want to preserve enough photos and memories to know who and what was important in our lives. For someone managing 25,000 printed photos, this advice was very reassuring.

In this same light, I don't feel like I have to track down every family lead or link to successfully preserve my family story and legacy. However, if I have easy access to existing information and photos, I do want to preserve what I can. Someday, I may wish to travel to Poland to track down my grandmother's roots and see where she lived. Or, my children might travel to Germany to see where their great-grandfather and his brother grew up; and then ended up serving on opposite sides of the First World War.

To keep the information straight and simple for one client with seven generations, we determined who was the oldest ancestor for which we had information, documents, or photos. I numbered that person or family as number 01. Each newer generation used the corresponding number. This system worked well.

Here's an example and screenshot using my own family:

- 01 Adalbert Kordus and Marianna Luczyk – my great-great-great-great-grandparents!

- 02 Stanislaus Kordus and Margaret (Swit) Kordus– my great-great-great- grandparents

- 03 John Kordus and Mary (Ritger) Kordus – my great-great-grandparents

- 04 Leo Kordus and Carolina (Lepak) Kordus – my great-grandparents

- 05 Stanley Kordus and Helen (Ostrowski) Kordus – my paternal grandparents

- 05 Stanley Kordus – just his photos

- 06 Jean (Kordus) Hartmann – my mother

- 06 Kordus Siblings – my mother's brothers and sister

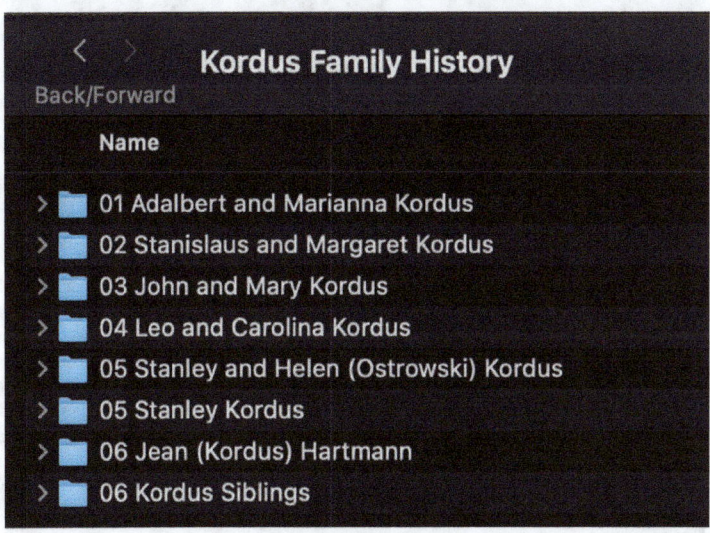

Later, I added a couple of folders in the system. Helen Ostrowski was my grandmother and we have several photo albums of photos she took when she was single. Those photos were scanned and put into a separate folder for her and designated with a 05, representing the fifth generation slot she shares with my grandfather.

I store my photos and documents in a FOREVER® permanent storage account. It is easy to add documents as I find them and share with family members. You can see the corresponding photo albums below to my folders in the previous screenshot.

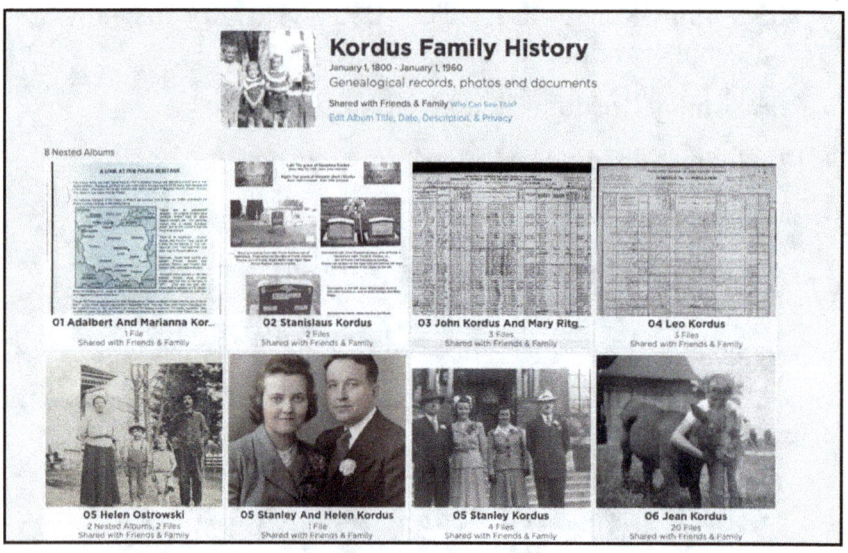

Since we don't use a standard genealogical numbering system at Pixologie, I thought it might be a good idea to learn more about the other systems for this book and avoid missing anything.

By good chance, my friend Mary Voell came to visit me at work. We started talking about what I was up to with this book. I explained how the genealogical numbering systems weren't working for me. Mary is a personal historian and has helped many people with their family trees.

Mary was delightful and said using a numbered pedigree chart was easy. I enjoyed hearing her explain more about how useful a numbered pedigree chart could be in organizing photos and documents. We drew the chart on a scratch sheet of paper. I could see how it worked and Mary mentioned that a normal chart reaches to the 32nd person, or the great-great-grandparent's position.

The numbering system starts with the first generation and works backward. I would be number 01 and so would my sister. Then, my father would be number 02 (males are always even numbered) and my mother would be number 03 (females are always odd numbered). I filled in all the spots I could.

My client had all of the names to fill in the spots. I thought, *Well, let me try it with my own family.* (I still have a lot of missing information to complete.)

My sketch is on the next page, using a nice form from Ancestry.com:

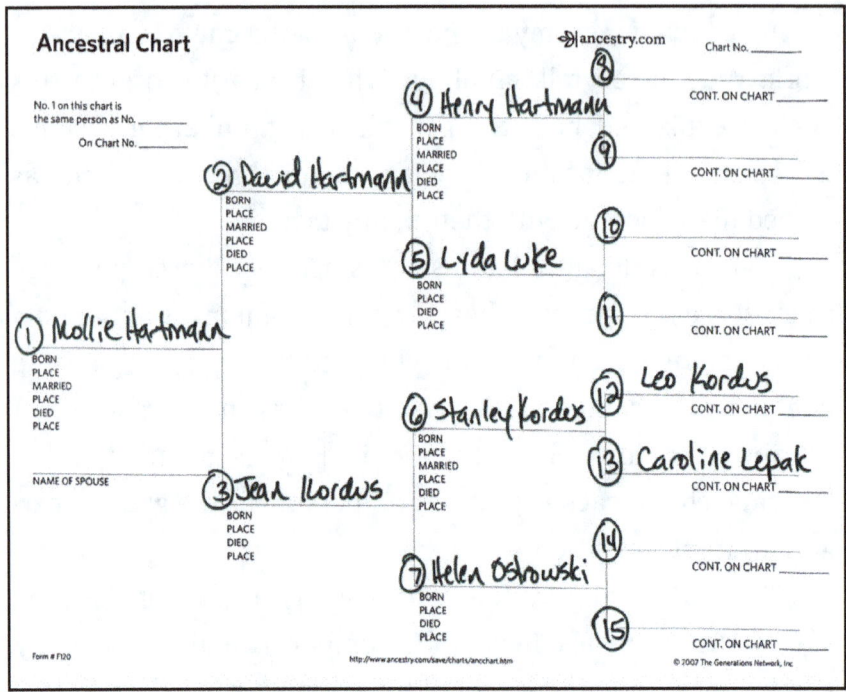

If I were to follow this numbering system for scanning photos and documents, this is what we'd have for digital folders:

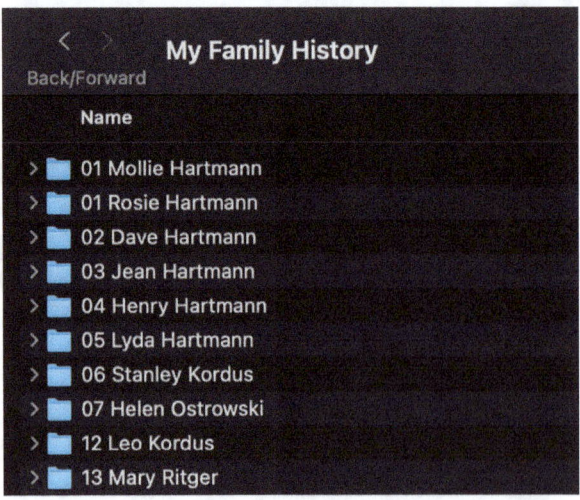

This chart is from my perspective and starts with my sister and me. However, I have no sense of who's who with this numbering system. Obviously, I know who my grandparents are, but the order here is confusing. It's also missing numbers for the names of people I don't know in previous generations.

I really want to understand the genealogist's mindset, but I can't balance this approach with having a neat and orderly system to see my family's materials organized and displayed.

- The numbering system does not tell me how many generations are represented at a glance. (Mary did point out that she could see the generations represented. As a personal historian experienced with family genealogies, I can understand this.)

- Six of the folders are empty. (This could motivate me to search harder for information about these relatives.)

- For my great-grandparents and great-great-grandparents, there just is not enough information, in my mind, to justify creating a whole separate folder.

- What if my 18-year-old daughter wanted to start this process? She'd have to start the numbering system over—with her being number 01.

Since developing our numbering system, we have used it successfully with other clients who have extensive family historical photos and documents.

Back to the albums in FOREVER numbered by generation. My family has access to these albums to download the photos and documents whenever they'd like. It's not a family tree, but I believe FOREVER allows me to present my family history in an organized manner. In addition, FOREVER continues to improve its services for users and I think we will see more features coming in the future that will help users preserve their family histories.

On the off chance that I did find additional ancestor information that came before my first identified generation, I would create a folder named 00 Earlier Kordus Ancestors. And it would look like this:

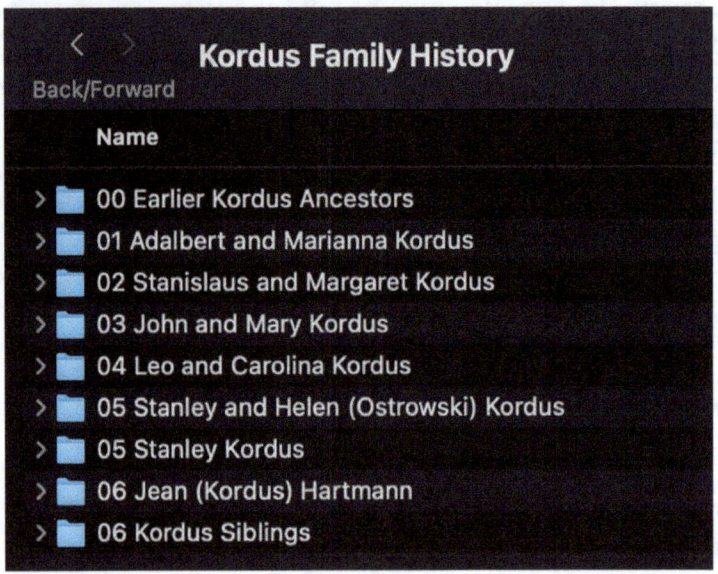

As I mentioned earlier in the book, you may be able to sketch out your family tree during your photo organization work. Names and dates are often found in old family photo collections.

Now it's time to transfer that information to a family tree program.

CHAPTER 8

CREATING YOUR FAMILY TREE ONLINE

You've organized and digitized all of the photos and documents in your family's photo collection. It's time to start working on creating your family tree if you haven't started one already with a site. Hopefully, you have a lot of notes to help you from the work you've done and the tree you have been sketching.

First question: What software should you use? You can purchase software on your computer or you can use an online service to build your family tree.

There are advantages and disadvantages to both options and we'll go over both. Either way, you'll be working with a standard digital family tree file called the .GEDCOM or .GED file.

GEDCOM FILE

GEDCOM stands for Genealogical Data Communications. GEDCOM was developed by The Church of Jesus Christ of Latter-day Saints to aid in family history research.

You'll want to be sure that whatever program/option you use, you can take your GEDCOM file with you. All genealogy software can open GEDCOM files. Some software programs have their own proprietary features. This means when you export your GEDCOM file, you may lose some of the functionality you had with a specific program.

For advanced users, you can even add someone else's GEDCOM file to your existing one. There are many resources out there to learn more about how GEDCOM files work. See the Resource section of a listing I have used.

Websites to Build Your Family Tree

Most people with any interest in genealogy are aware of Ancestry.com, the granddaddy of all family tree and history websites. If you like being connected to the Internet for the closest access to clues, information, and distant relatives, you'll enjoy the websites available.

Ancestry.com

Because of my clients, I was already familiar with using Ancestry.com. I started putting my family tree together in Ancestry. It was exciting to see how much was already available on my family. Because there are so many people using Ancestry.com, you'll find information, records, and even possibly photos for some of your ancestors.

Here's a screenshot of my family tree:

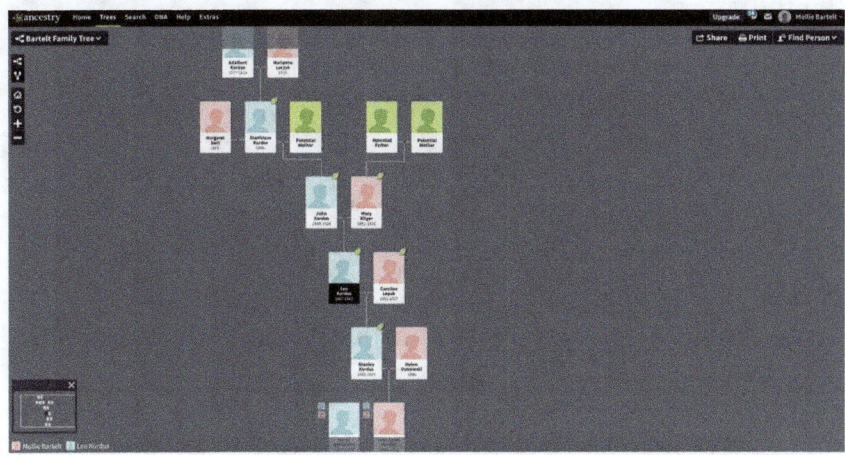

The green highlighted boxes and leaves indicate that Ancestry.com has identified potential hints and additional ancestors for me. I simply have to click and explore the hints to learn more!

Users can change the family tree layout with the options at the top left in this screenshot.

I enjoyed searching for records to help fill in the gaps. Here's a section of the 1900 US Census, which contains Leo Kordus's family, along with some additional information.

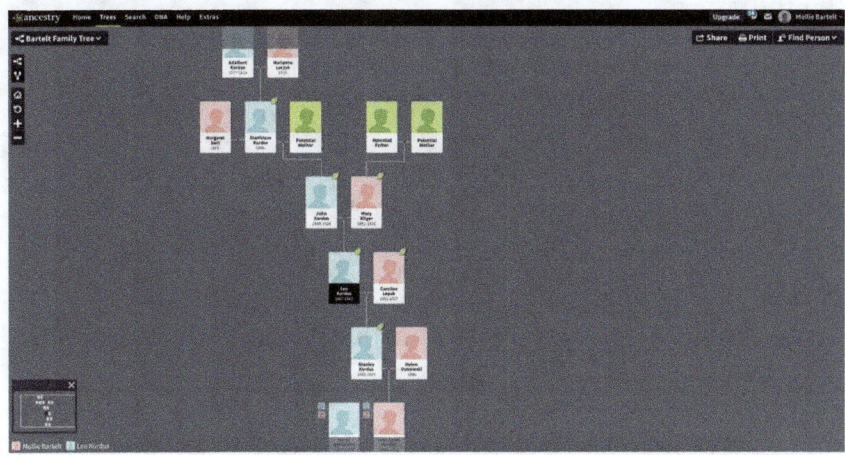

Before starting this journey, I never knew the name of my grandfather's father, much less his grandfather. I downloaded this document from Ancestry and saved it with the other documents on my computer. I also uploaded the census to my

FOREVER account so I could easily share it with the rest of my family.

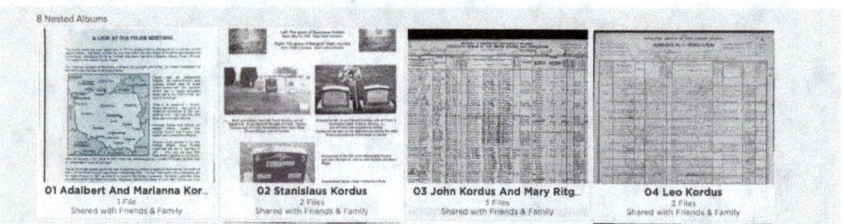

Even though I have no photos for John and Mary, I do feel like I have a connection to their lives.

Look at some statistics from Ancestry's website:

- In 2017, Ancestry generated more than $1 billion in revenue
- Ancestry has more than 3 million paying subscribers across all its family history websites and over 30 billion records from more than 80 countries.
- AncestryDNA has more than 15 million people in its consumer DNA network, making it the largest in the world. (1)

Ancestry.com provides you with dozens of hints for your family tree, some of which may or may not be accurate or even for correct individuals in your tree. Some hints lead to different people with the same name. You'll have to investigate some of the hints. Sometimes the hints link to outside websites for which you need a subscription as well.

Be careful! The hours speed by when you are investigating your family tree hints! I have to put a timer on so that I don't lose my whole day in the project.

During your work, I think it is well worth a monthly subscription to download immigration documents, census records, view other family trees that might overlap with yours, and much more. Ancestry.com costs around $24.99 per month to start with other payment options available to save money. However, I don't know if this is the final place to build your family tree.

You can print your family tree and family group sheets, even if you don't pay for the Ancestry subscription. Most importantly, you can export your Ancestry GEDCOM file and store it on your computer.

Steps to Download Your GEDCOM File from Ancestry

1) Step One – Go to your settings and click on Trees

2) Step Two – Click on the tree you wish to download

Settings	Your trees
Your Account	These are trees that you've created.
Public Profile	
DNA	
Trees	
Communications	Trees shared with you
Help	If others share their trees with you, they will be visible here.

Tree name	Date modified	Role	
Bartelt Family Tree	8/7/2021	Owner	>

3) Step Three – Click on Export Tree

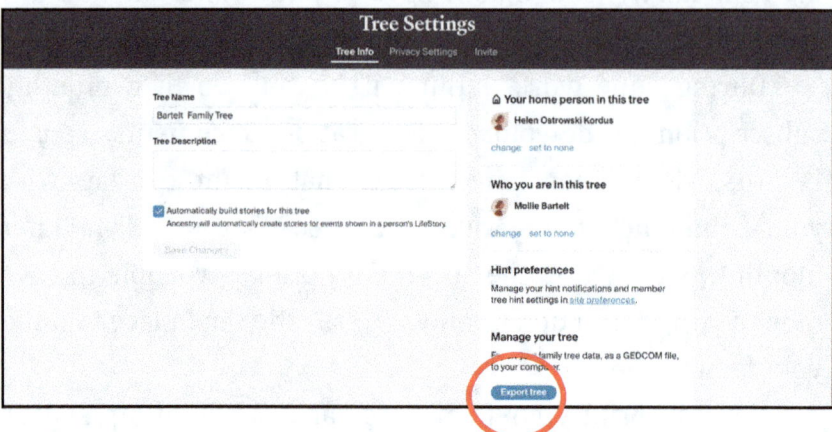

4) Step Four – When your GEDCOM file is ready, click the download button.

Manage your tree

Export your family tree data, as a GEDCOM file, to your computer.

⬇ **Download your GEDCOM file**

download tips ⌄

For my purposes, I created my first GEDCOM file in Ancestry and then downloaded it to my computer to test with other sites and software.

FamilySearch

FamilySearch.org, run by The Church of Jesus Christ of Latter-day Saints (LDS) in Utah, provides you with another genealogy resource for gathering information and building a family tree.

FamilySearch believes that "every person deserves to be remembered." This site offers the largest online family tree. It's home to information about more than 1.2 billion ancestors. When you build your tree here, you are helping to contribute to this community effort of remembering countless people over many generations. As a community-building, one-world family tree, every one does have access to edit and change information. This can be frustrating when the information you find might conflict with information you currently have about your family.

Tyler, our Pix Technician, pointed out to me that there are billions of records available here, but they have not all yet been indexed to be searchable.

I did not find the tree builder as easy as Ancestry's. Here is a pedigree view of my mother's side of the family.

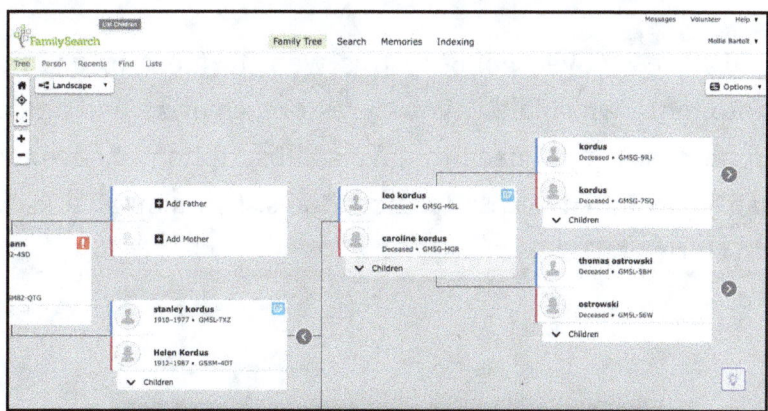

If you need more help with FamilySearch.org, you can visit a FamilySearch Center at many of the local churches. See the Resources section for a link to find one near you.

Family Search is completely free and only requires you to create an account to access its records and resources.

MYHERITAGE.COM

At MyHeritage.com, you can create your tree, test your DNA, work with old photos, and even narrate a life story.

I uploaded my GEDCOM file to this site and here's what the full screen view looks like:

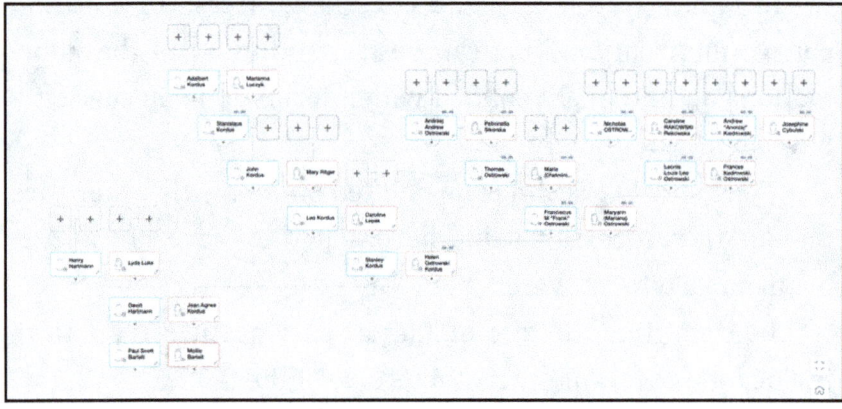

I have enjoyed going to this website more to use their photo tools, which allow you to restore, colorize, and animate old photos. You do need to have a subscription to have more than just limited access to these tools. (An annual subscription starts at $129.)

Here's a screenshot of the photos I have uploaded and the enhancements available. All of this work is done using artificial intelligence (AI) technology to improve your photos. You get results in less than a minute!

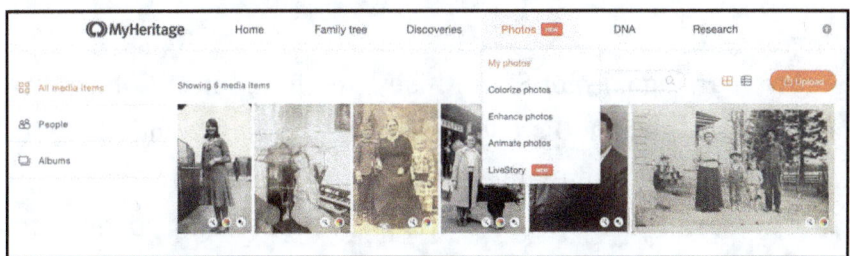

And, you can download the photos and GIF (your photo animation files) from the site. Your original photo is pre-served, in addition to the enhanced photo. With the paid subscription, you can download the photos without the MyHeritage watermark.

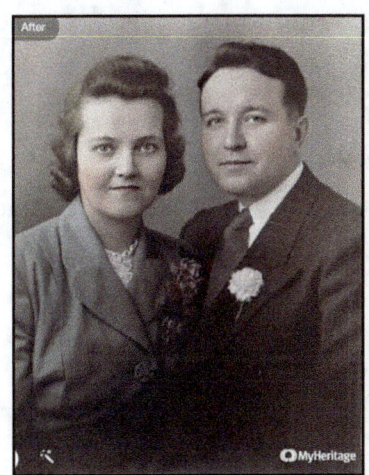
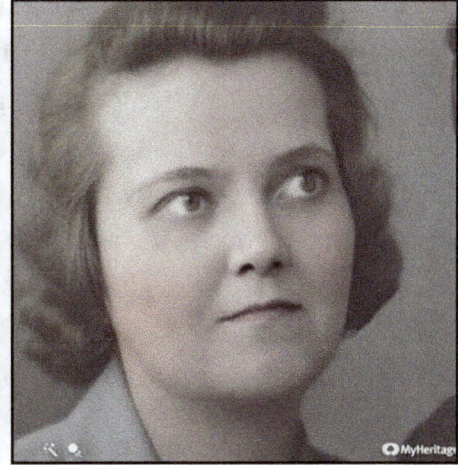

See my grandmother looking away in this screenshot
of the animation MyHeritage did!

Okay, to be honest, MyHeritage's photo tools are a complete rabbit hole that could distract you from getting the important stuff done. I know, because hours can fly by when you see what it can all do!

COLLECTIONAIRE

A few years ago, I met Stan Kinsey, the founder of Collection-aire. He's a former Disney executive who has founded three additional tech companies, and he is his family's curator. Kinsey saw there was a better way needed for people to consolidate all the different online places that photos, videos, books, and documents were stored. He developed Collection-aire to allow people to have their own controllable, secure, enhanced, personal ancestry that will leave an amazing legacy for their families.

Collectionaire is a simple but smart cloud app for building the ultimate collection of a family's history and best memories, including digital photo albums, home movies, digitized scrapbooks, slide shows, audio recordings, journals, etc. It's not a photo storage site, but instead a "hub" that complements cloud sites like SmugMug, Flickr, Google Photos, Apple Photos, Vimeo, YouTube, etc. by aggregating all your media into one easy-to-navigate site via your family tree.

Kinsey writes,

> "Your family's history includes more than just your ancestors... it also embraces the special memories of your immediate family. Create a beautiful online private collection of your entire family's history and best memories,

including photos, home movies, audio recordings, journals and documents, using Collectionaire. Then connect and share your collection with young and old, who easily and intuitively find every memory via your online family tree."

You can start by importing your GEDCOM file or by manually building the current portion of your family tree with immediate family and maybe going back a couple of generations, depending upon how deep you have rich memories, especially videos, newspaper articles, etc.

Then you can start connecting the photo and media accounts to each person's story and then presented in Collectionaire. You'll want to review your links to ensure they continue working properly as time goes by.

You don't move, import, or store your photos and videos in Collectionaire. Instead, you'll store them in one, or several, cloud photo and video sites of your choice and then presented in Collectionaire.

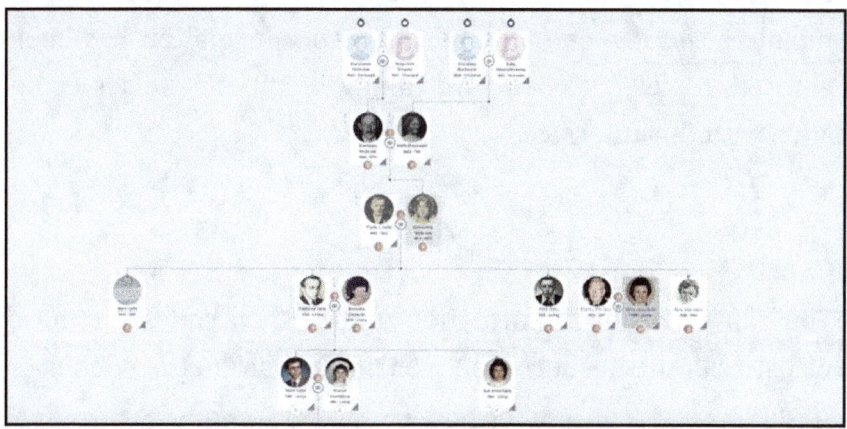

Our client Gen's family tree in Collectionaire.

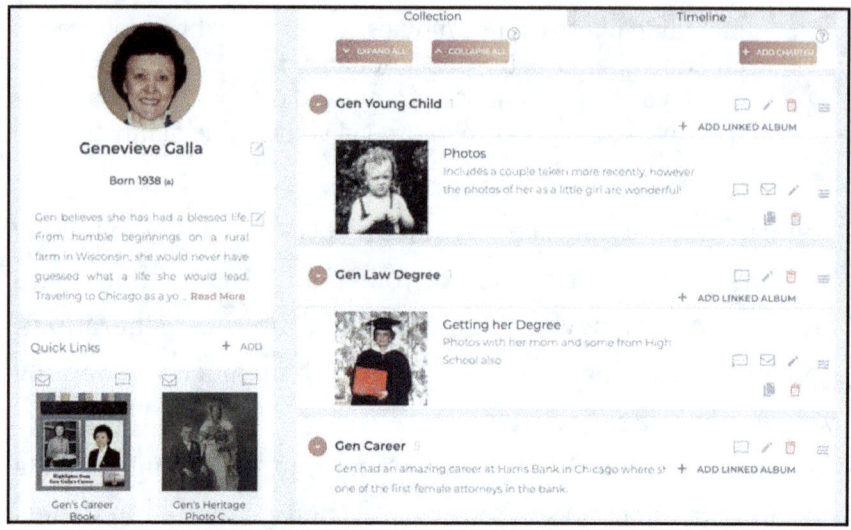

When clicking on a family member's profile, you can view the person's history and photo collection links.

This is Gen's media collection that we helped connect to her Collectionaire account. When you click on her in the family tree, you can view the items in her media collection.

Gen's photos and video are primarily being stored in FOREVER, but linked here through her Family Tree in Collectionaire. You can see how much more information has been entered. It's easy to see your family member's stories come alive with this interface.

You can find more information and coupon codes for these websites in the Resources section in the back of the book.

CHAPTER 9

CREATING YOUR FAMILY TREE ON YOUR COMPUTER

The safest option to creating and/or managing your family tree is to create it on your computer with a downloaded program. This way, even if you don't have access to the Internet, you can continue to work and have access to your tree. You also don't need to wade through all the hints and clues from the online sites, which can be inaccurate.

Remember, we always recommend backing up your computer files keeping a copy at home and a copy outside the home. This second copy could also be made to a cloud backup like Backblaze, Microsoft OneDrive, iDrive, or a Dropbox account.

CHOOSING A PROGRAM

If you search online, you can find both freeware or shareware genealogy software, in addition to software that you can purchase. There are so many options that I had to look at reviews to know where to start. Features that you will want to consider include:

- Availability of a free trial
- Compatibility for PC or Mac, depending on your computer
- Ability to import and export GEDCOM files
- Integration with Ancestry.com; FamilySearch

In the reviews, Legacy Tree Maker, Family Tree Maker, and RootsMagic come up consistently in the Top Ten. However, Legacy Tree Maker is not Mac compatible (I use a Mac) so I looked at Family Tree Maker and RootsMagic. You can also search for reviews online to make your own decision.

FAMILY TREE MAKER

Family Tree Maker sells for $79.95. (1) It originally was sold by Ancestry.com, which retired the program back in 2015. Another software company, Mackiev, purchased the program from Ancestry and relaunched Family Tree Maker in 2017. It does not offer a free trial. Features include color coding, ancestry hints, themes, dozens of charts and reports, and more. There are add-ons and educational content you can purchase as well.

Our technician Tyler prefers using Family Tree Maker and he provided me with this screenshot of my family GEDCOM file imported and displayed.

Family Tree Maker syncs with your FamilySearch and Ancestry accounts for easy importing, ancestry hint investigation, and more.

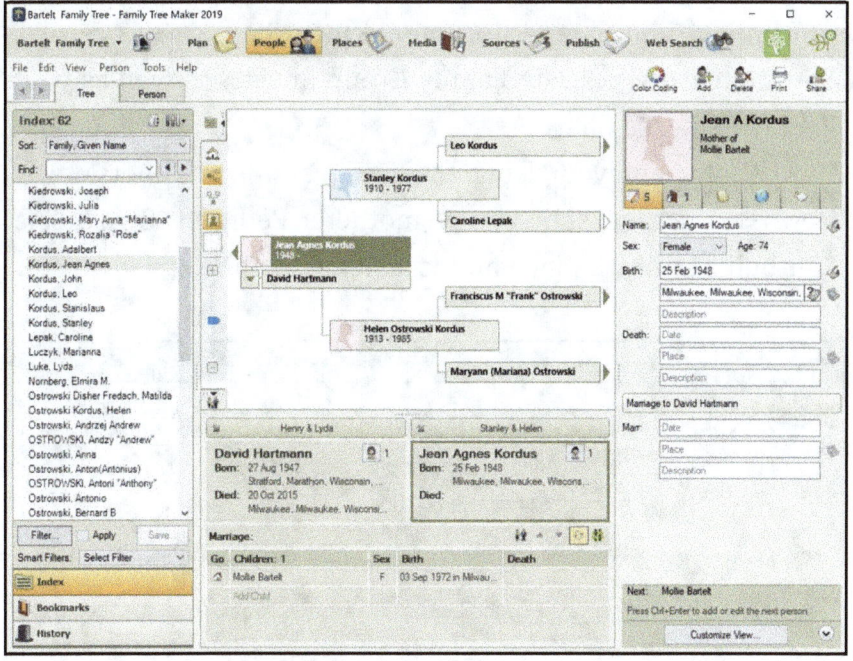

RootsMagic

RootsMagic is available in a free version and the full version sells for $39.95. (2) Within five minutes, I was able to import my GEDCOM file that I had downloaded previously from Ancestry and see my family tree. (Alternatively, if you are subscribed to Ancestry.com, you can connect RootsMagic and import it directly from Ancestry.com. You can also connect to FamilySearch.) You'll get to see the Ancestry hints right in RootsMagic and click on them. You will need to provide your login credentials for Ancestry and FamilySearch to have access to those sites.

When you click on a family member, you can enter all the pertinent dates and information about that person. You also can import photos and documents into the person's record. You can easily generate Family Group Sheets, as well as your Family Pedigree Chart.

I really enjoyed using the free version of RootsMagic. Here is a screen shot of my mother's Pedigree Chart. The lightbulbs indicate that a hint is available online.

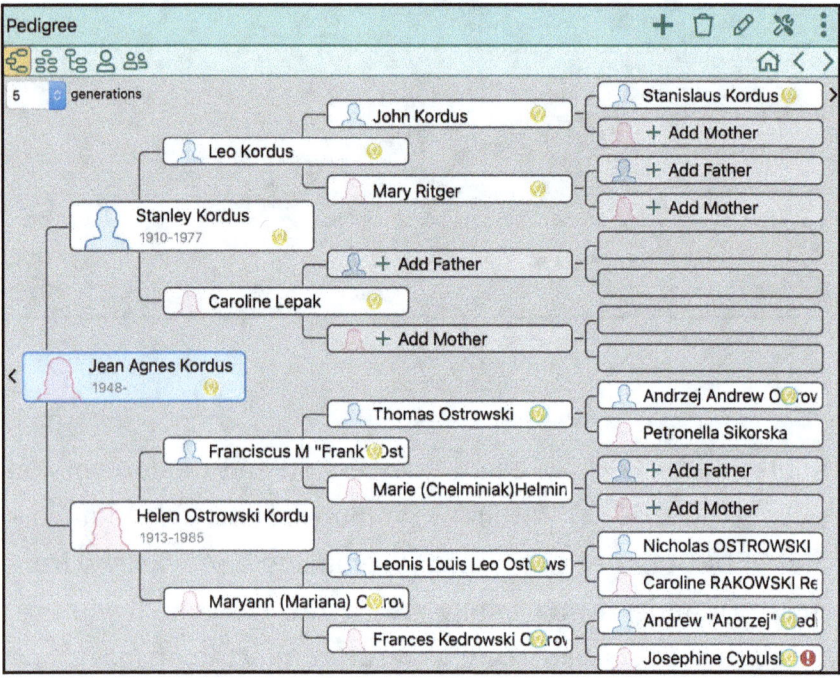

I would highly recommend that you read the reviews and download the free trials to help determine what genealogy program will work best for you. Then, spend money on a program when you are sure you will stick with the family research.

CHAPTER 10
WEBSITES AND PLACES FOR ADDITIONAL RESEARCH

While there is a lot of information on the big family history websites, those sites incorporate hints from many other sources. Some of these sources you can research on your own. Whenever you find a document, be sure to download and save it to your computer. It can be challenging to find it again online.

PASSENGER RECORDS

Do you have ancestors who emigrated to the United States from Europe? There is a good chance there may be passenger records of their travel.

It helps to know the dates of immigration. Most likely, arrivals occurred at Ellis Island, which operated from 1892 to 1954. Prior to that, immigrants arrived through Castle Garden.

Remember my grandfather's passport mentioned earlier in this book? With the information of the date issued and his full German name, I was able to search the Ellis Island records and find his documents.

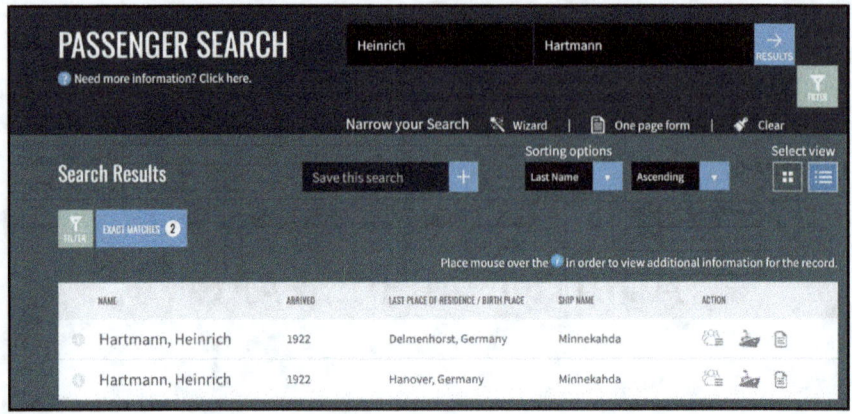

In the Action column on the right side, I viewed the original record, information about the boat, and was able to order prints of the documents.

Here's the passenger manifest:

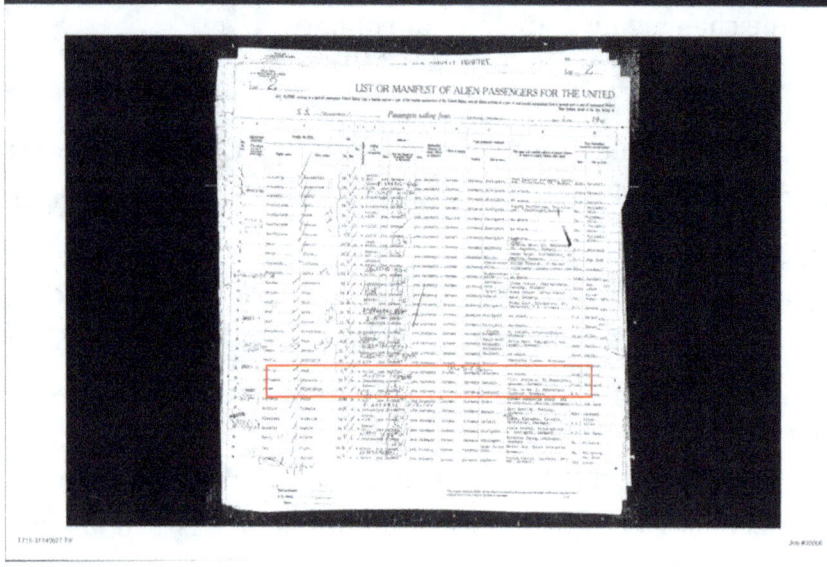

FIND A GRAVE.COM

If you happen to be on Ancestry.com and there's a photo of an ancestor's grave, it may likely be linked to Find a Grave's website.

Here's some information about Find a Grave from their website:

> "Find a Grave got its start in 1995 when founder Jim Tipton built a website to share his hobby of visiting the graves of famous people. He found that many people shared his interest and quickly opened the site for all individuals (famous and non-famous) with a mission for finding, recording and presenting burial and final disposition information worldwide."

In 2013, Find a Grave became a wholly owned subsidiary of Ancestry.com. The site continues to be free to use.

I searched for my great-grandmother's grave and found it within a few minutes. If your family member happens to be in the collection, you can click on their link and see their grave photo and information. If available, the listing will also show family members.

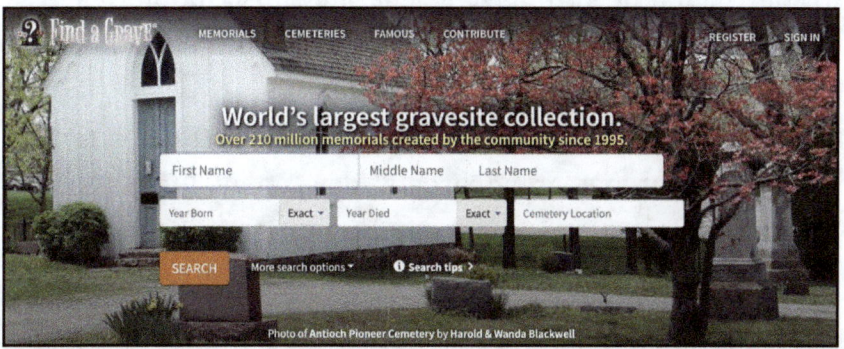

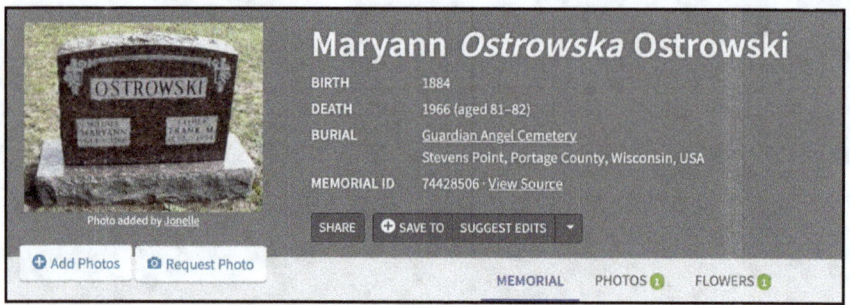

You can download the listing's photo or add your own additional photos. Sometimes the image is of low quality. However, you now have the exact location if you wish to go visit your ancestor's grave sites.

In addition, some users add photos of ancestors along with obituaries. You can also click on the cemetery name to see who else in your family may be buried there.

NEWSPAPERS.COM

Want to know if your ancestors were in the newspaper at all? I love Newspapers.com, and originally accessed it through Ancestry.com with their hints.

I quickly found out that I needed to subscribe to read the newspaper articles. Even though Ancestry already owns this resource, you need to have a separate subscription to access the news articles. It is around $20 per month or $75 per six months.

For my mom's side of the family, I was so excited to find articles about my grandparents' day-to-day life. With the subscription, you can download the articles as JPGs or PDFs. There is an easy clipping tool to select what you wish to save.

A wise person told me that family history is never done. There are always new things coming to light (a new record) or a family member suddenly finds items to share (photos, audios, videos, newspaper articles, etc.) Family reunions are good places to find such treasures. When you find information, be sure to print it out, as well as save it to your computer. It may not be there when you come back.

In this article, Frank Ostrowski's name is highlighted in yellow and I learned that my great-uncle Barney returned to town to enter a seminary school! Believe me, I know enough of my mom's history—he was never a priest!

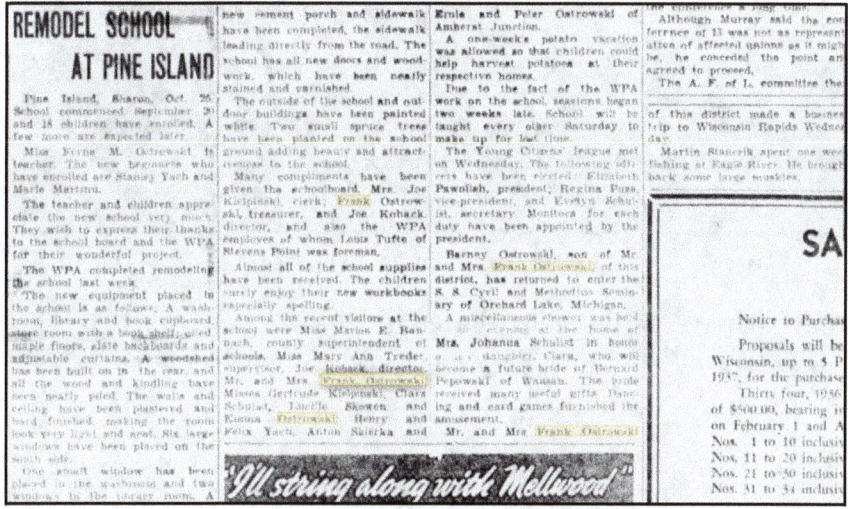

I also found this article about my grandmother's brother, who tragically died after a home explosion. This story was so newsworthy that Newspapers.com had it listed in many

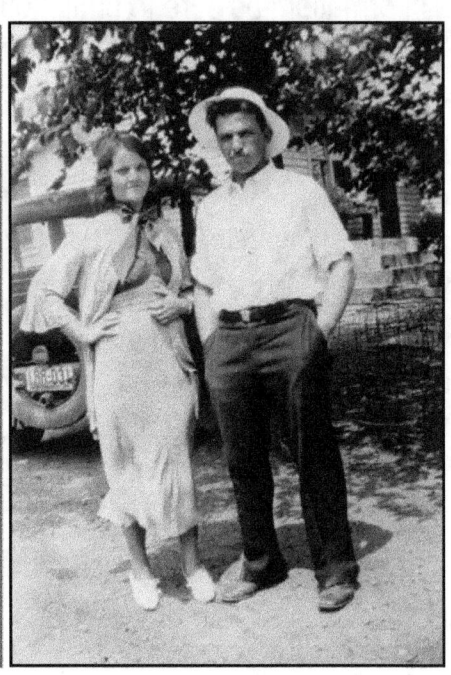

Fatally Injured by Explosion of Tank

MILWAUKEE (AP) — Herman Ostrowski, 52, of suburban West Allis, was injured fatally Thursday night when a tank, described by authorities as a home-made still, exploded in the basement of his home.

Ostrowski was taken to a hospital where he died of abdominal injuries.

Lt. Edward Thompson of West Allis police said Ostrowski was using an acetylene torch to repair a 55-gallon drum that contained mash when a combination of gasses caused the explosion.

My grandmother and Uncle Herman

newspapers throughout the country—see it was written by the AP (Associated Press) back in the 1950s.

What an amazing resource to continue connecting people in our families to the stories of their lives!

Newspapers.com offers over 300 years of newspapers from small towns to large cities from across the US and world. They keep adding more as well.

FOLD3.COM

Do you have a relative with a military history? This website, also owned by Ancestry, offers millions of military documents to help track your ancestors who served. It, too, requires a subscription. I have seen them offer three days for free around military holidays and the website offers a seven-day free trial.

The Fold3 name comes from a traditional flag folding

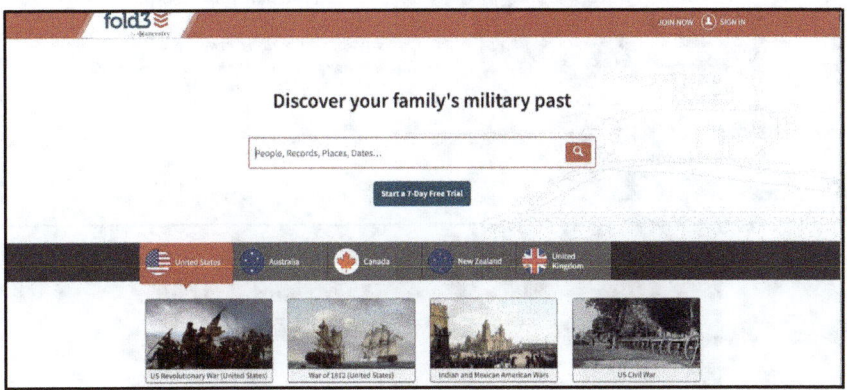

ceremony in which the third fold is made in honor and remembrance of veterans who served in defense of their country and to maintain peace throughout the world.

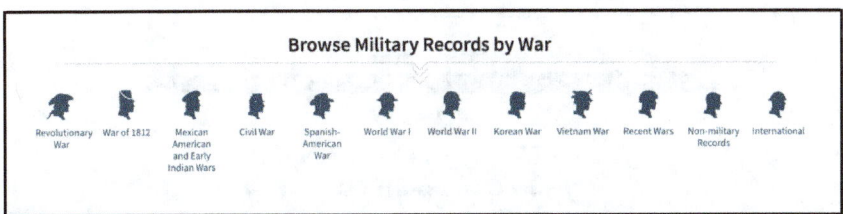

This is the home screen from the website:

Fold3 offers US military documentation from wars going back

Date		Name	Hometown		
164 Oct 10	Do	Cap Mitchele	Acquackanonk	Do	24.7
166 Oct 12	Do	L. Halsey	Morris	Do	3.15
170 Nov 11	Do	Cap Debow	Minisink	Do	21.9

Joseph Halsey's name listed on US Revolutionary War Rolls - Lt. Halsey from Morris

Ledger found in American Revolution records

It says "To Cash borrowed of the following Person's visit in February 1777. Joseph Halsey 2730.

to the   Revo-

GRAVES REGISTRATION CARD HAMILTON COUNTY CINCINNATI, O.

Name	HALSEY, JOSEPH, JR.
Address	" "
Date of Death	1796	Place	Cincinnati, Ohio
Cause		Date of Burial	1796
Date of Birth	1751	Place	Springfield, N.J.
Name of Cemetery	Not Known	Location	" "
Lot No.	Section No.	Block No.	Grave No.
Marker: Flat	Upright	None
Next of Kin	(W) Mary Halsey

SERVICE RECORD Official Ohio Roster states buried in Hamilton Co., Ohio

War Served In	Revolutionary
Date Enlisted	Date Discharged	Serial No.
Branch of Service	Rank	Sergeant
Company, Outfit or Ship	Eastern Bn., N.J.

fold3

Joseph Halsey Jr. Grave Record from Cincinnati Ohio

The websites mentioned here contain information only as good as what has been able to be saved, digitized, and catalogued in their databases.

For myself, I was hoping to find information about my great-uncles' service in World War II. However, there were no records available to view or download for them. And, many people interested in their family's military service are in the same boat for an awful reason.

In 1973, a disastrous fire occurred at the National Personnel Records Center, destroying over 15 million official military personnel files. The archives.gov website reports that 80% of Army personnel records were destroyed for the enlisted who were discharged from 1912 to 1960 and 75% of Air Force personnel records were destroyed for those discharged from around 1947 to 1964.

This was a terrible loss for our nation and for many, many families who wish to know more about their loved ones' service.

Hopefully, you have been able to put together enough details to learn about your ancestor's service to our country. It is certainly important to preserve that history and legacy.

BUREAU OF LAND MANAGEMENT (BLM)

Did your ancestors help settle the West? The Bureau of Land Management has many records of land being given or sold to settlers. They:

> "provide live access to Federal land conveyance records for the Public Land States, including image access to more than

five million Federal land title records issued between 1788 and the present. We also have images of survey plats and field notes, land status records, and control document index records."

Land purchased by our client's ancestor in 1885 during the settling of the West documented in this Land Patent.

OTHER ONLINE RESOURCES

The websites I have listed so far can only offer so much information, documentation, and photos. You may want to research more about your family history or go even further back.

Around the world and here in the United States, local organizations have archives that might have some of your family information. In some instances, you might find a personal narrative that someone has written based on a shared branch of your family.

Be sure you copy the websites you find into a document and print the information you want. Even better, save the information or webpage as a PDF on your computer for easy access down the line.

This is important, because sometimes you might find an obscure website that is helpful. Finding it again might be difficult.

In our project work, we have used many different websites, a few of which are listed below. As you search, you will find a variety of websites about your own family lineage, possibly hundreds of places to look!

- My Pomerania – German & Polish Family Database
  https://mypomerania.com/databases/

- New York State Family History Records
  https://www.newyorkfamilyhistory.org/online-records

- History of the Sikora Family in Milwaukee
  http://baillod.com/main/sikora.html

- My Halsey Family History
  http://rochistory.com/family/halsey.htm

Your job will be to filter through all of the available information and compile things that support your family history.

You can keep downloaded information in the same folders as the photos you have for the different generations of your family.

And, as you search, you'll find that time flies super-fast! Just mentioning it again. It may help to put a timer on so that you don't become so enthralled that you all of a sudden realize eight hours has gone by! (Been there myself!)

DNA RESEARCH

Another way to research your ancestry is to have a DNA test done by one of the family history sites. Ancestry.com has the largest consumer database and its DNA tests include:

- DNA results of origins and ethnicity from over 1,500 regions, sometimes down to a city
- Pie chart and percentages of your ethnicity estimate
- Depending upon your regions, a timeline of historical changes with expert-curated content
- Potentially how and why your family moved from place to place around the world
- DNA matches – connect with others who share your DNA
- Discover individual traits influenced by your genes

Ancestry's DNA tests start at under $100. You can search online for other providers and see what they offer. The two others that come to mind include 23andMe.com, as well as MyHeritage.com. Watch for sales around the holidays.

One other site used by genealogy researchers is FamilyTreeDNA.com, which was founded in 2000 and is also a pioneer in the field.

LivingDNA.com is another site based in England. This may be more helpful if you have African or English ancestry.

About seven years ago, my sister and I had our DNA testing done through a Groupon special. Back then, it cost a couple hundred dollars to do the testing, so my sister bought the test for me as a gift. This is the only graphic I have saved from when I logged in to see my results!

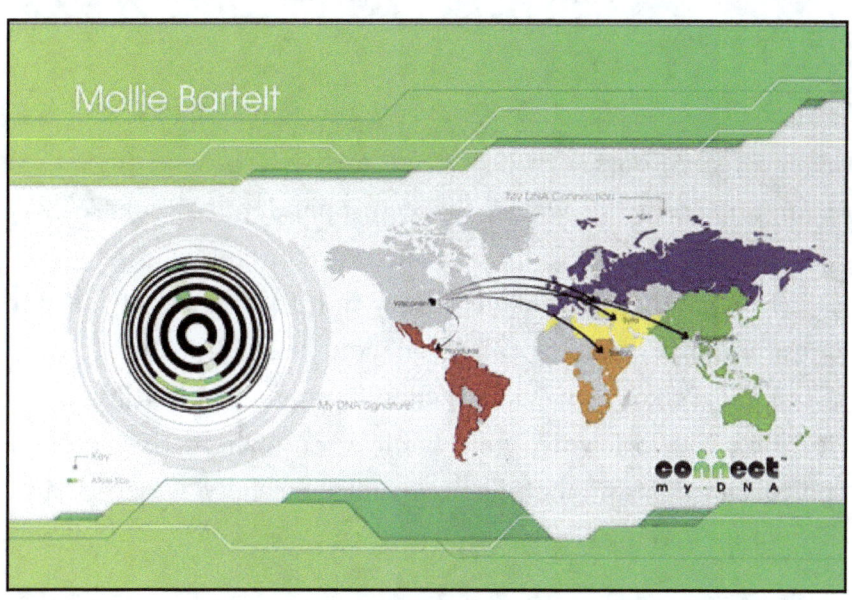

Of course, since then I lost my login and I believe the company was bought out! I'm not even sure what this all means. So, the moral of the story—save your results in a PDF on your computer!

And, maybe don't use a Groupon special!

Just remember, you are sharing very personal, private health information with large, global corporations. Of course, these companies have extensive privacy policies. You should review how your DNA data could potentially be used and what your DNA data might possibly reveal.

In the Resources section, I have a link to a *Consumer's Advocate* article entitled, "Best DNA Testing Based on In-Depth Reviews" (7) that may be of assistance to you.

Some of the companies will allow you to upload a previous test from another company. This may help you find more DNA matches.

ROOTSTECH

Every year, RootsTech hosts one of the largest genealogical conferences in the world. Since the pandemic, RootsTech is completely online and the education is completely free!

Browse their extensive library to find all sorts of recordings on any genealogical topic you need. It is hosted by FamilySearch.org (previously mentioned as a potential online location to work with your family tree) where they aim to unite families and help people discover new ways to find ancestors and preserve family history.

PLACES TO DO RESEARCH IN PERSON

Despite the billions of digitized records, they represent a small fraction of the records around the world still in need of digitization.

If you live in the area where your ancestors settled or if you can travel to where they settled, you may enjoy researching in person. This can happen in your area or all the way around the globe! Here are some ideas of where to go:

- **Local historical societies** – You can see what photos, documents, and more might be on hand. Some of these societies do have online databases for you to search. Definitely call ahead to ensure the hours of operation and that someone will be available to help you.

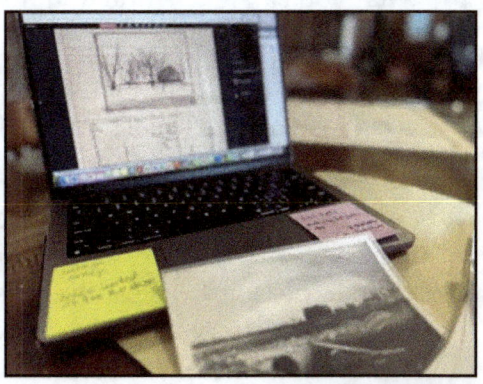

I visited the Milwaukee County Historical society to see if I could find any more photos of my grandparents farm. It was a long shot, but we found a construction photo of the road they lived on. The farm in the photo was next door to my grandparents. Thankfully, someone had written on the back of the photo where the photo had been taken!

Although it wasn't what I really wanted, this photo gives me an idea of what life was like and what the land looked like back in the 1960s. Today, the landscape is full of restaurants, businesses and more.

(Photo used with permission from the Milwaukee Historical Society)

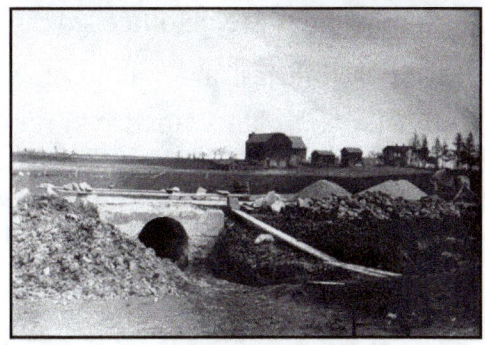

> **VERY IMPORTANT!**
> When you find information, be
> sure to print it out, as well as
> save it to your computer. It
> may not be there when you
> come back.

- **Libraries** – Check out what is available in your library. At Pixologie, we frequently do community presentations in libraries and have seen often that the libraries have historical photosnewspapers, and documents on file. In large urban cities, the library may have huge repositories of genealogical information available. Spend time seeing what you can learn, find and investigate.

- **Churches** – If you know the church where your family was a member, reach out and see if the church has any physical archives you can access. Many, many churches have records that have not been digitized yet.

- **Cemeteries** – We've already discussed how you can find your ancestor's graves with FindAGrave.com. Go visit them in person. This can be meaningful and you never know what else you might find in the church or town where the cemetery is located. If the cemetery is large enough to have an office, go there first.

The possibilities are endless! Search online, make your contacts, and plan your travel! For some, this involves international travel to go to a family's roots in another country.

HIRING A GENEALOGIST

If you do travel to another country, I highly recommend you work with a local genealogist who knows the area well, speaks the language, and can help save you time, effort, money, and frustration. And that leads me to the option of hiring a genealogist to do more research if you are still looking for answers.

We'll hear about Gen's story at the end of this book. Her cousins traveled to Poland in the 1990s to learn more, but they could only go so far. Gen wanted more in-depth history going a couple of generations further back. My colleague Caroline Guntur assisted with hiring a local Polish genealogist to assist Gen with deep research into her family's past that was still uncovered in her ancestor's homeland.

This can be an expensive proposition where tens of thousands of dollars are required to find more ancestral information. In other countries as well as our own, many documents are buried in church and local government archives. Doing such research requires travel, time, the pouring through and photographing of many old documents and papers, and translation of those documents. Sometimes, the search ends when the researcher finds the necessary records were water-damaged centuries ago or have simply gone missing.

You can find genealogists online who are willing to do the research for you. I would definitely recommend getting references from anyone you might consider hiring.

FOREVER, the photo storage company I mentioned earlier, also offers genealogy research services and will upload documents directly to your FOREVER account for you.

That said, most of our clients interested in family research are content to gather what they can through the resources I have listed in this book. It's fascinating to learn about what is all available out there to help us in the discovery of our family history.

HIRING A PERSONAL HISTORIAN

If you need full assistance in preparing your story for publication, consider hiring a personal historian. He or she will help you organize your thoughts into a meaningful narrative. You can find many resources on the Association of Personal Historians' webpage. (Although the organization folded in 2017, their resources are still available today.) They write:

> "Looking for a powerful way to connect generations and preserve memories? Think about creating what's known as a personal history. It could be a memoir, a family biography, an oral history, a legacy letter, or another tribute, and it could take the form of a printed work, a video, an audio recording, or other formats. Whatever form of remembrance you choose, a personal history can have a profound impact on your life and the lives of your loved ones."

Please see the Resources & Reference section in the Appendix for the web addresses for all the resource websites mentioned in this chapter.

SECTION THREE

CLIENT STORIES, COLLEAGUE CONTRIBUTIONS, RESOURCES & REFERENCES

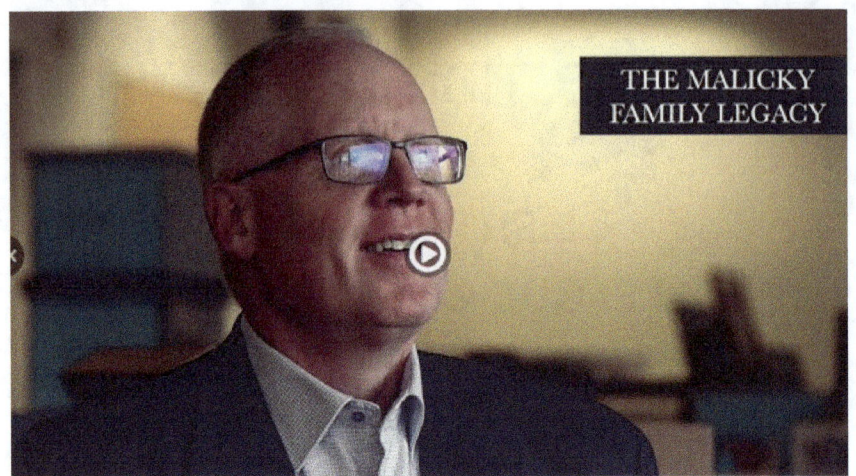

Use the QR Code to hear Eric Malicky's message to his family
and future generations.

When your family photos and materials have been organized and preserved, you can
use QR codes to connect people to the stories and so much more.

CHAPTER 11
CLIENT STORIES

MORE THAN JUST A FAMILY LEGACY PRESERVED

Back in Christmas of 1985, Eric Malicky gave his family two photo albums filled with many family memories. He wrote a note, "These photos made me more aware of how fortunate we are to have each other." His parents and two brothers spent time paging through the books and having fun with reliving family stories.

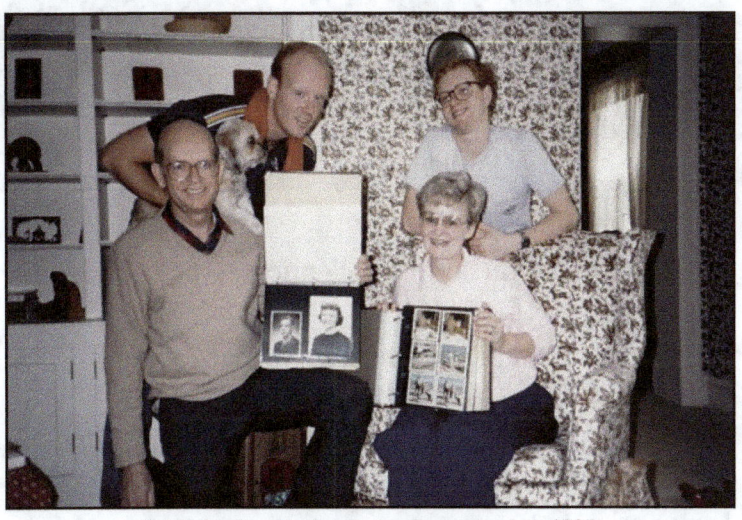

Eric's family with the photo albums back in 1985

Twenty-some years later, Eric inherited back those albums, along with the entire Malicky photo collection. This included over 160 years of photos, documents, scrapbooks, albums, envelopes, and much more. Armed with technology, he was determined to preserve their family history.

Over the next few years, Eric spent time scanning some of the photos, but didn't have a final strategy to manage the photo collection once and for all. A busy orthopedic surgeon, Eric also didn't have the time to figure it out. He stored all of this collection in heavy-duty, extra-large bins and decided to get help.

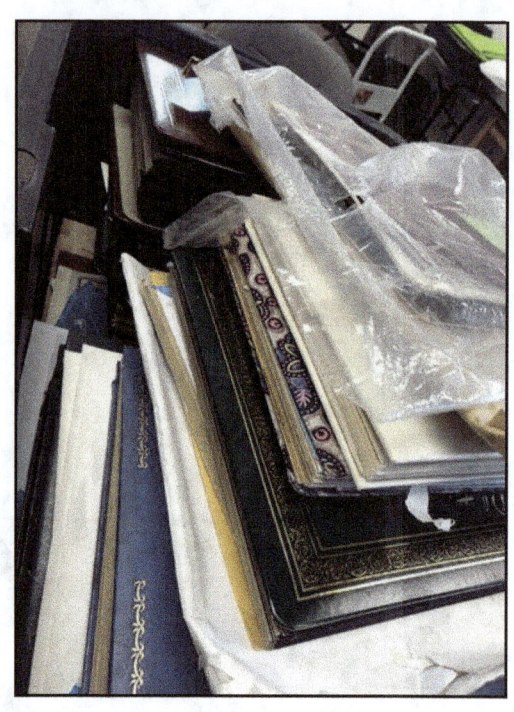

After our first meeting, we sorted the family collection, which included:

- Documentation and photos of maternal ancestors dating back to the 1500s in England
- Information about being the 14th descendent of Thomas Halsey, one of the founders of the Southampton Colony in New York, 1640

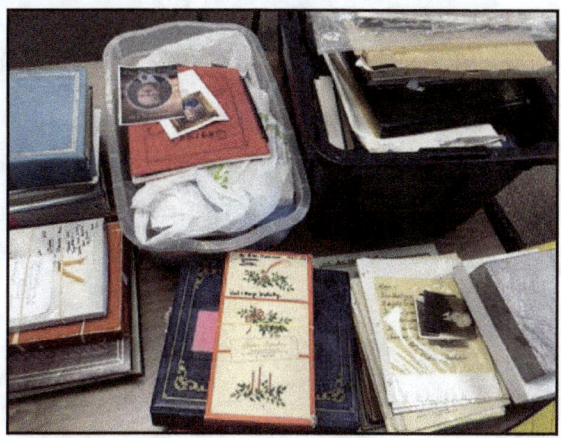

- Photocopied photos of ancestors named Vencil Malicky (pronounced Malichkis) who immigrated in the 1800s from Bohemia and Czechoslovakia

- Fascinating booklet, original articles and photos of a 1920s-era professional baseball player

- Details about how family had to move frequently during the Depression

- Fragile, crumbling scrapbooks of college days in the 1950s full of photos, sorority news, and more

- 16 reels of film of life in the 1960s –never seen and were going to be thrown away

- Photos, newspaper articles, audio of Neal Malicky, President of Baldwin Wallace University

- Grandma Malicky's sticky photo albums

- Six albums with Eric's maternal side history, the Wilson family

- Countless memories of what life was like growing up through the years

GETTING STARTED

With a few basic notes taken during the first meeting, we began to see the family tree emerge. Eric had a lot of information already. Using our basic system of sorting photos by family and then by decades, we came up with a game plan including:

- Organize the heritage photos by family group, generation, and decade
- Remove photos from albums
- Remove duplicate and repetitive photos
- Review the memorabilia and scrapbooks, identify important pieces to preserve
- Digitize the reel-to-reel film and audio reels
- Scan the photos into sensible digital folders
- Create a FOREVER online photo archive for the family photos and media
- Upload digital photos from folders to corresponding albums
- Add descriptions, names and details to the photos in the online photo archive

Eric agreed and we went to work. Over the course of a summer, we worked on the different pieces of this project. As we found memorabilia and notes, we were able to complete the family tree with dates, more names, and information. Eric periodically checked in, brought additional photos and information sent to him from his Aunt Joyce to help build the photo archive.

Some of the photos would not come out of the sticky albums and therefore had to be flatbed scanned. The majority, however, were able to be scanned with a high-speed scanner.

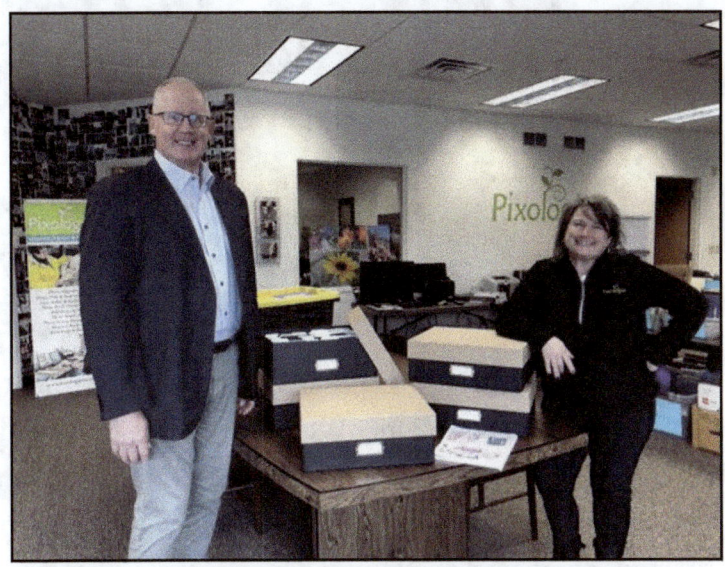

Eric and Pixologist Mollie Bartelt with his five archival boxes containing all his family photos, film, and documents.

CREATING THE ONLINE PHOTO ARCHIVE

On the next page, you can see the Malicky History Album in the FOREVER online photo archive. Eric's family history can be traced back 14 generations on the Halsey side. I numbered the Halsey Family as 00 in the naming system because there were no photos or documents of the generations in between Thomas Halsey and Addie Reed besides Vencil and Antonia Malicky.

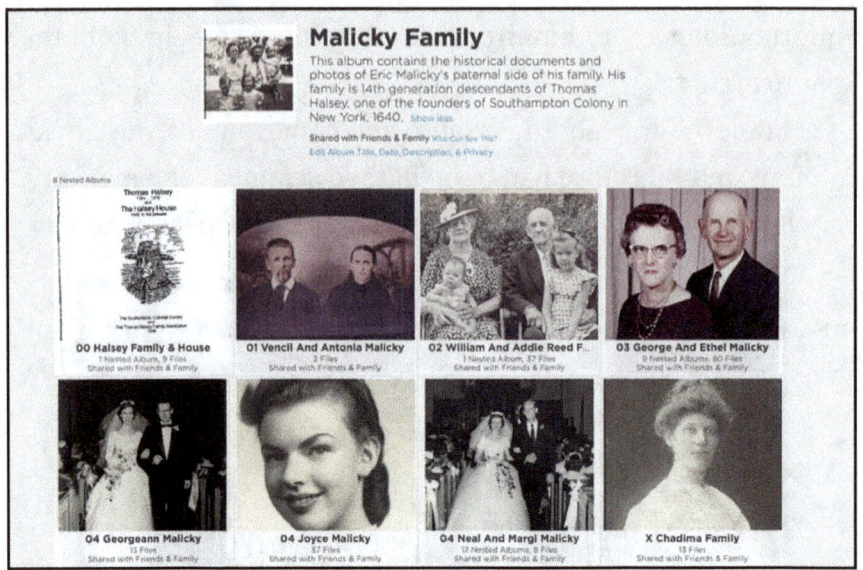

Within 03 George and Ethel Malicky, we find "George's Baseball Career" nested album. We scanned one article dated in the 1970s. It provided a lot of information, including that George played baseball from 1923 to 1934 when the Depression started. Years ago, the family had created a document on George's baseball days. We scanned the 54-page booklet, along with the original newspaper articles. Someday, maybe his story will inspire a future Malicky descendent to play a professional sport! (shown opposite)

Eric's parents, Neal and Margi, have 17 nested albums, including their early years, wedding, having children, careers, and much more (shown opposite).

By clicking on the nested album "Neal Malicky Career," we can see photos, audio, and newspaper articles spanning his professional life. Neal inspired many, many people through

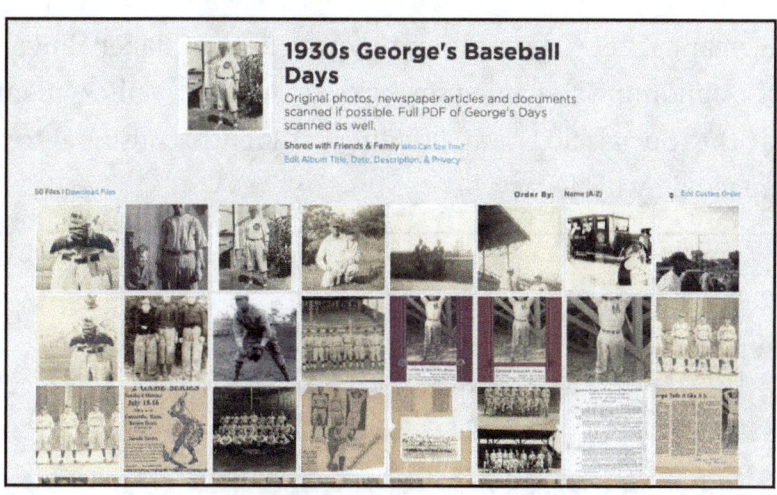

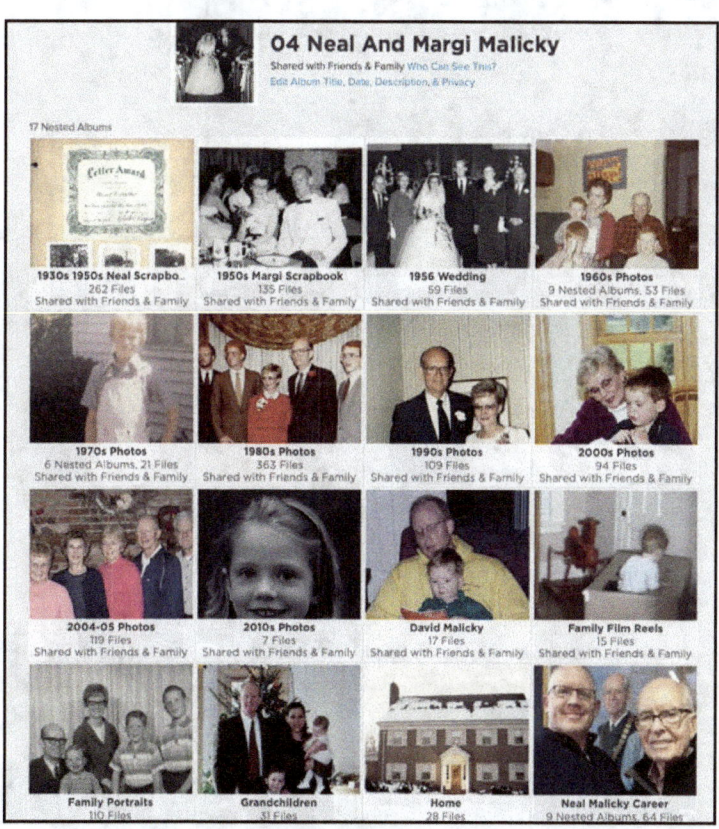

the years. After his retirement as president of Baker University, a building was named for him. At the Neal Malicky Center for the Social Sciences building, students continue to be impacted by his legacy.

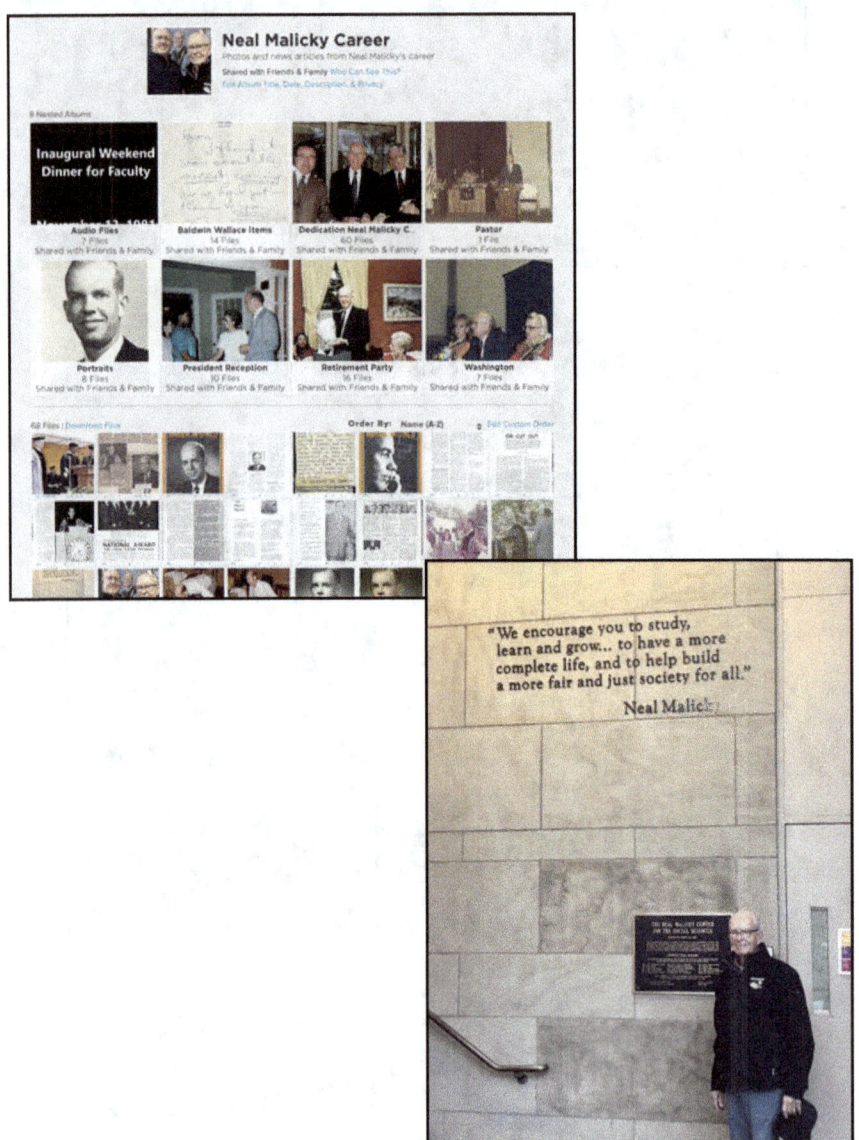

Eric's commitment to his family history ensures that the family values of hard work, persistence, and helping others will be passed on to future generations. With our assistance, Eric also compiled "The Malicky Family History," a treasure for his family.

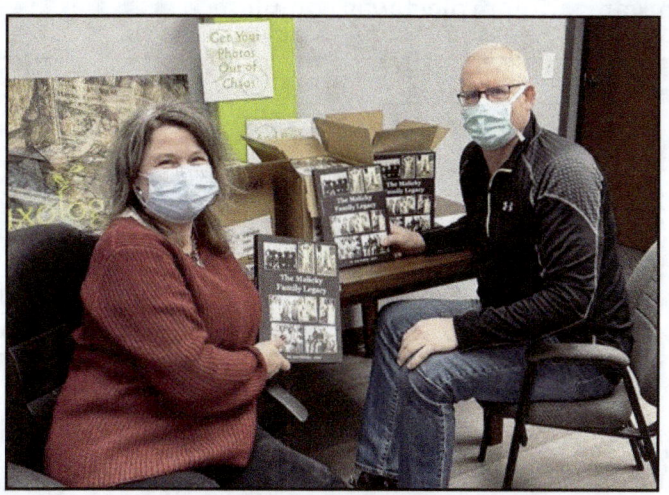

Below, pages from "The Malicky Family Legacy"

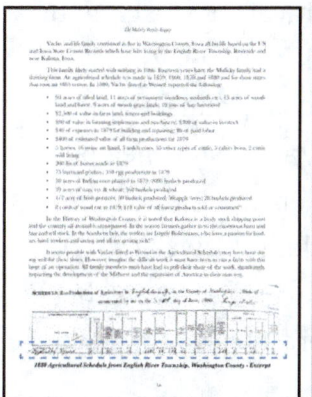
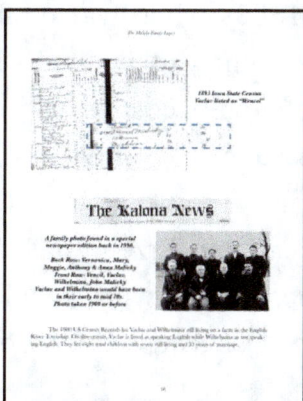
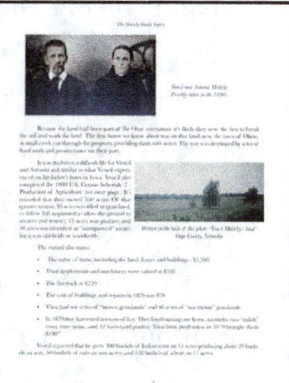

GEN GALLA - MY FAMILY STORY HAS BEEN TOLD

Gen Galla was featured in *The Pixologist's Guide to Organizing and Preserving Your Family Photos* and discussed above. At the age of 78, Gen hired us to organize her collection. After Gen saw her completed photo estate project, she told me, "You have restored my life."

Here's a screenshot of the organized albums after Gen's photo organization project was complete:

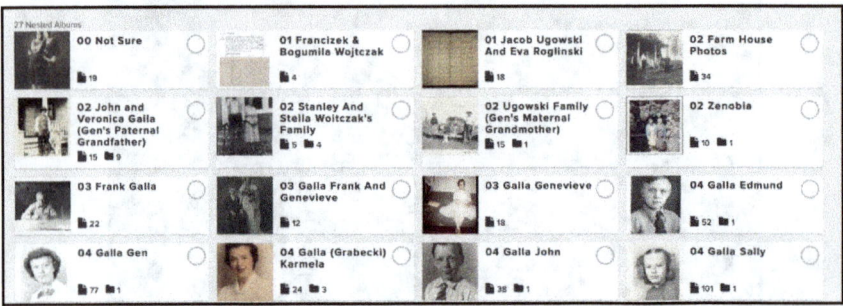

This certainly appears to be a comprehensive family archive.

But Gen wasn't done ... she was determined to get to the root of her ancestors, wanting the names, details, and history of her great-great-grandparents. Her Polish ancestors lived in Poland during the 1800s when war, political interests, and turmoil had split the country up in many different ways.

For this work, we enlisted the help of Caroline Guntur. She connected us to Your Roots in Poland, a Polish genealogy company with researchers able to help Gen track down her heritage. Senior researcher, Przemysław Jędrzejewski, Ph.D., worked in Chmielno, Koscierzyna, Czaple Nowe, and other locations in Poland. (1) Because the records were not digitized yet, he photographed the pages from the record books to get them back to Gen.

Here are two of the original records of her great-great-grandparents' marriages:

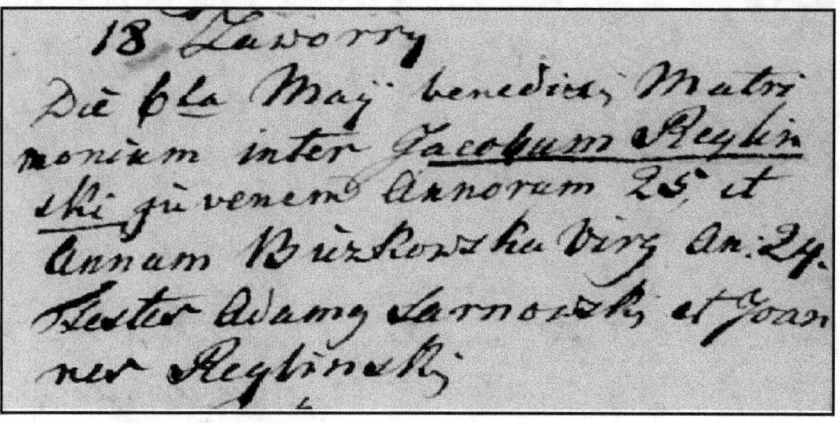

1822 German Marriage Record of Jacob Reglinski and Anna Biczkowska

1844 August and Marianna Galla (Galecki) Marriage Record

Here are the marriage records for Gen's great-grandparents, Jacob and Eva Ugowski:

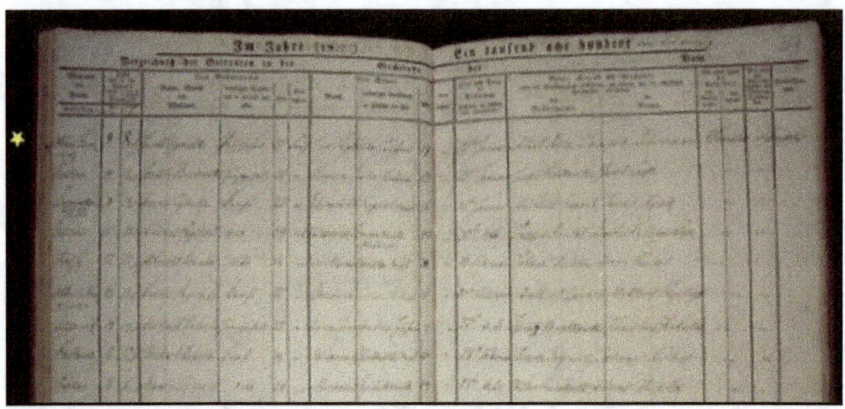

Marriage record of Jacob Ugowski & Eva Reglinska - Chmielno - Jan 17th 1843
source: Archives of the Pelplin Diocese - Book W192 - picture No 0039 - record No 8

Residence of the bride	Number in the parish where		Groom				Bride				Place and day of marriage (with the digit and spelled)	Surname, status and place of residence except declaration of consent, parents as well as potential carers of groom's/bride's side		Place and number of the announcement		Surname of the priest who gave the wedding	Remarks
	the marriage took place	the marriage announcements took place	Surname, status and place of residence	Previous marriages	Age	Confession	Surname, status and place of residence	Previous marriages	Age	Confession		groom	bride	groom	bride		
Abbau Brodniz	8	8	Jacob Ugowski	Bachelor	27	Catholic	Eva Reglinska	Virgin	17	"	January 17th	Albert Stolz	Joseph Lehmann	Chmielno		[unreadable]	

Jacob Ugowski married Eva Roglinski in 1843.
Above photograph shows their original marriage record
Below, a translation of the marriage record.

Because the researcher conducted his investigation right in the areas these families lived, we were able to learn that the Ugowski and Reglinska families were listed in several records. It's possible that Jacob and Eva may have grown up together.

Gen's entire family came from the area that is Poland today. In the 1800s, that area was often under turmoil and land borders changed between Prussia (Germany), Russia, and Austria. Her photo collection included letters written in the 1940s and 1950s by her Polish extended family. These letters included pleas for money as life was quite poor for the Polish people. All of these photos, letters, maps, old records paint a vivid picture of what life in Poland was like through the 1800s to mid 1900s.

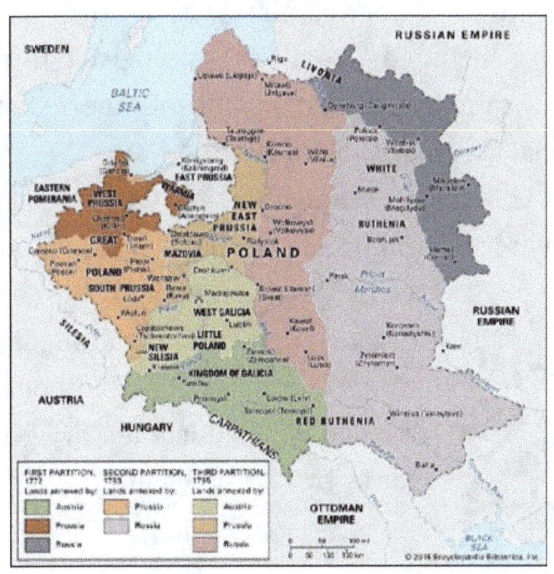

Just one of several maps in Gen's family history files.

Gen continued her genealogy journey after her photo collection was organized and saved. With all of this additional work, Gen preserved her family's history, spanning more than eight generations. What a tremendous gift for the future generations of her family to know their Polish roots.

KIRA HENSCHEL FAMILY LEGACY

You are reading this book because of my book publisher Kira Henschel and our first conversation together about five years ago. She instantly saw the relationship that photos have to family history and thought a book about bringing photo organization and genealogy together would be an excellent resource.

She had a personal reason for her interest as well. Kira had inherited all of her parents' and grandparents' photo collection. Kira's father's family lived in Europe. Her prestigious history included two anesthesiologist parents, a Noble Prize winner in physics, and significant other educational and professional accomplishments.

Kira's collection of materials was vast—from old photos, frames, oversized and fragile certificates, and much more. We were proud to help her manage the organization and curation of her collection. You can learn more about her project by watching a documentary film produced for us by Matthew Peters.

QR code for documentary
film about this project

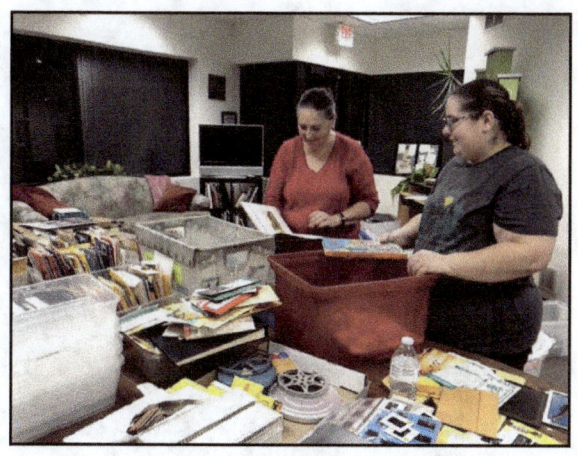

Kira and her daughter initially tried to start the organization on their own at our offices during a group event where people could come to our studios and work on their own projects. It was easy to see that they might be in need of some help!

Kira allowed us to take over the project and in short order, we had divided up her materials by media type, decades and major categories.

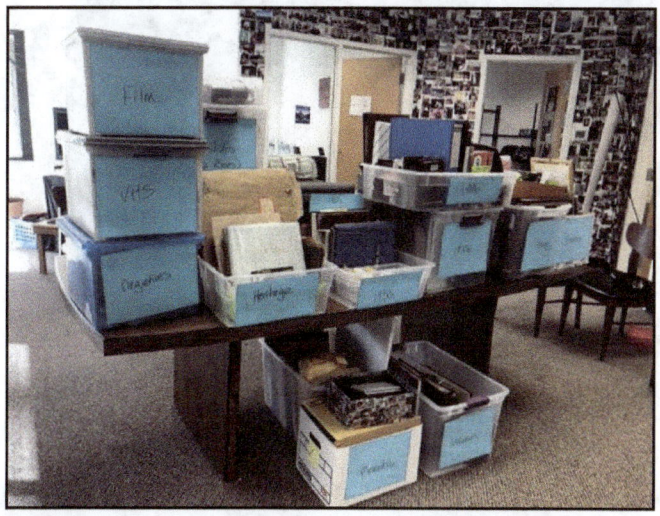

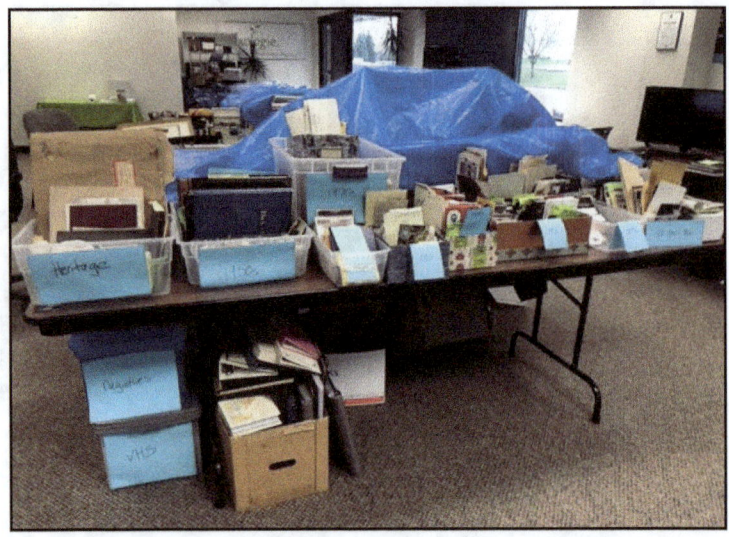

Here you can see we've started breaking down the major categories into subcategories and years. It's fun to see how the boxes and bins start reducing down as we removed unnecessary items.

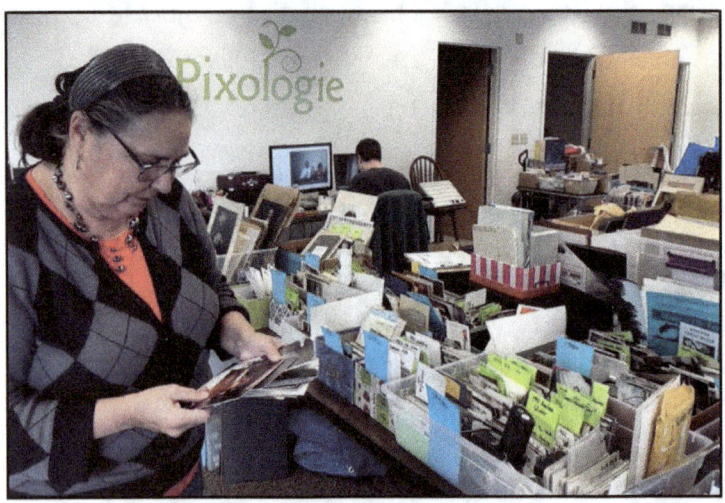

Kira inspecting her family photos, answering questions for us during the organization process.

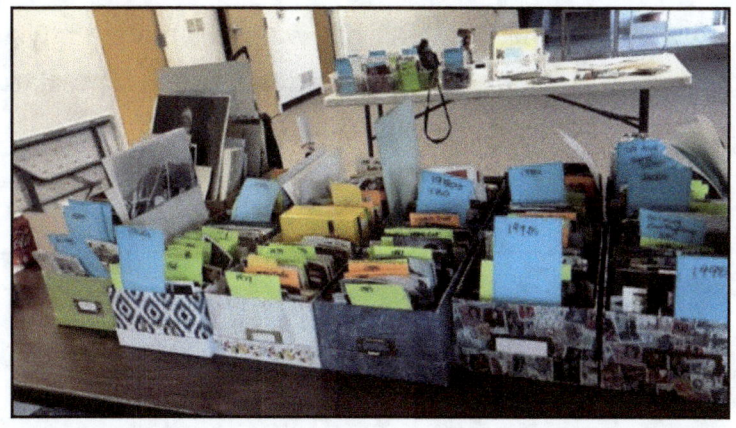

We finally ended up with about 11,000 photos here in these boxes and they were ready for the third sort by month, event or sub-subcategory. Eventually, we scanned around 9,000 photos, slides, documents, and more. All of these digital files were uploaded to Kira's FOREVER account, where she can easily share them with her family and knows that the Henschel legacy is preserved and safe for generations to come.

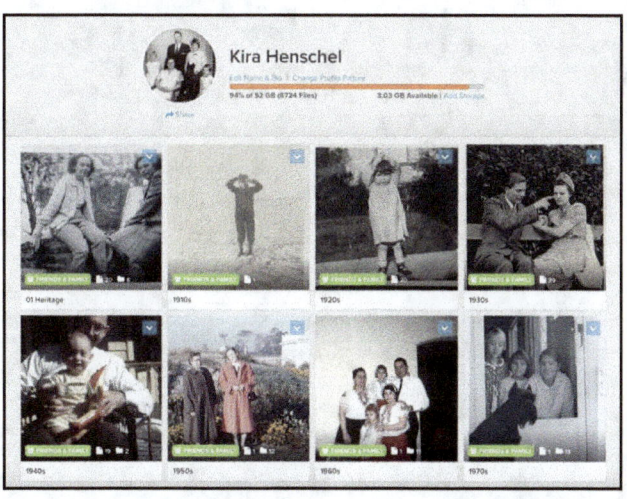

Kira's father, Ernest Henschel, was a prominent physician and his materials are preserved. Her mother, Ann Bardeen Henschel, was an equally prominent physician.

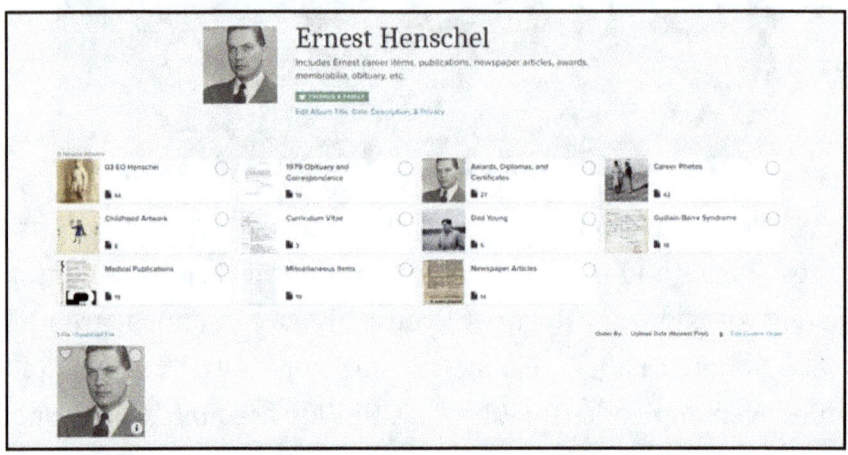

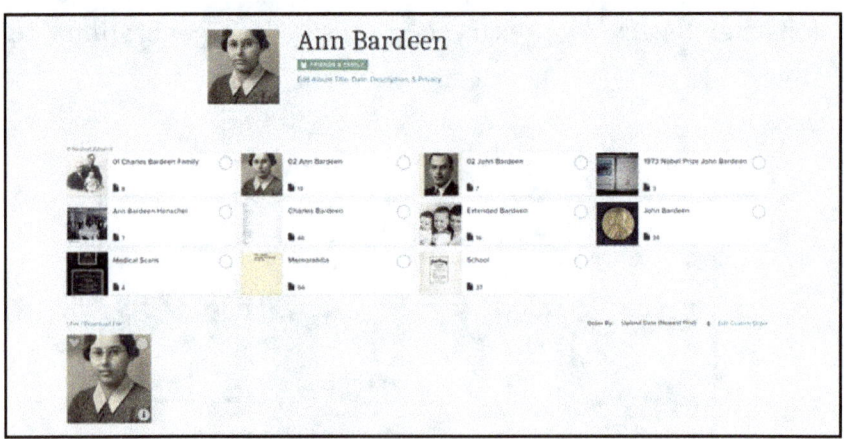

Kira now has photos identified and easily accessible for when she is ready to work on her genealogy.

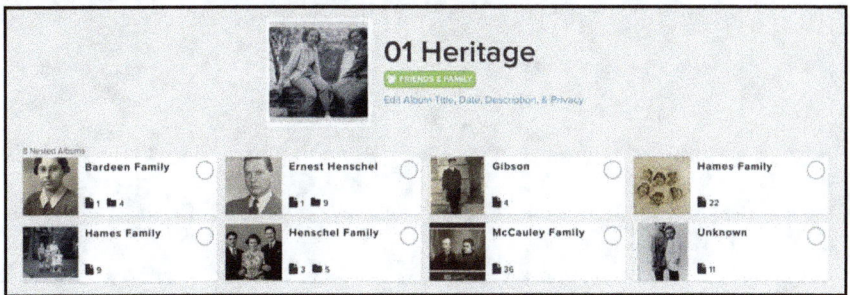

CHAPTER 12
COLLEAGUE CONTRIBUTIONS

I have had the good fortune to meet many interesting people who also are on the journey with me. In this chapter, I am thrilled to provide you with another perspective from someone who works with deep family research for her clients. Caroline Guntur is "The Swedish Organizer" and a colleague I rely on for genealogy research when my clients need it.

10 STEPS TO START YOUR GENEALOGY JOURNEY
By Caroline Guntur

Tracing your roots has never been more popular! From DNA testing to shows like *Finding Your Roots* and *Who Do You Think You Are*, family history has finally gone mainstream, and it's now America's favorite indoor hobby. Never before has it been so easy to discover new connections and unlock family secrets.

It can be both challenging and scary to embark on this type of journey because you don't know what you're going to find until you start looking, but I can promise you that no matter where it ends up, it'll be a deeply rewarding experience.

So where do you begin? Here are a few steps to get your started:

STEP 1: WRITE DOWN WHAT YOU ALREADY KNOW

The first thing you should do is write down what you already know. You probably already have the basic information you need to get started, such as your own name and birth date, your parents' names, your grandparents' names, and so on. If you or another family member have been adopted, you may face some additional challenges in uncovering this type of information, but any details you have will help. You need a place to start, even if it's only with one simple fact. As you begin to compile these details, questions will inevitably start to emerge. Write them down. These are your research questions, and should be approached one at a time.

STEP 2. ORGANIZE YOUR INFORMATION

As you start to collect information, you'll need to stay organized, and setting up a system right away will help you be more efficient in your research. Decide if you want to keep your information digitally, or if you'd rather go the old-fashioned route and use a pen and paper. Both ways work just fine, but understand that as you continue to gather information, it'll get harder and harder to keep it all organized. If you're set on working traditionally, get a set of dedicated binders right away. If you'd rather go the digital route, invest in a software, like Family Tree Maker, Rootsmagic, or Legacy.

It may be a small out-of-pocket cost, but it will be invaluable tool as you continue on your journey. Preferably, you want to keep this information on your computer to start.

A common rookie mistake is to just start a tree online, and then end up merging it with incorrect information. Take my word for it and start your journey in an organized manner. You'll be glad you did!

STEP 3: DON'T JUST SEARCH, *RESEARCH*!

Genealogy works best when you ask a specific question and find the answer to it before moving on. This is known as "focused research," so choose your first research question and set out to find the answer to it. A good question will be, for example: "Who were the parents of my great-grandfather John Smith, 1848-1903?" instead of something like "Who were the ancestors of John Smith?" The latter will have too many answers, and it would not even be clear which John Smith you're talking abou—remember that there could be multiple generations with the same or very similar names. Once you have ONE solid question, it's time to start digging.

STEP 4: INTERVIEW YOUR FAMILY

Before you look for any official records, ask your relatives if they might have something to share. More often than not, your family is sitting on a goldmine of information, like old photos and documents. The older generation may remember a great deal that you've never heard mentioned before, and you don't want to miss out just because you didn't think to ask, so pick up the phone and reach out!

STEP 5: GO ONLINE

A good place to start looking for records is online. There are minimal costs involved and it's a good place to start exploring because you can do it from anywhere. You'll want to look for reputable sources that can give you more clues about where to find copies of your family's original documents.

Two great places to start are Ancestry.com and FamilySearch.org. When you find information on your family, make a note of the source citation, so that you can look for the original document if it's not yet available online. If and when you find that original, make a copy of it, record the information, cite it, and file it for future reference.

STEP 6: VISIT A REPOSITORY

Digitization projects are well underway all over the globe, but unfortunately, it will take decades before even a fraction of the world's documents will be available via your computer. This means that many of the documents you need will be tucked away in an archive somewhere. If you live in a different state or country than the one your ancestor lived in, it may be a bit trickier to get your hands on this information, but there are plenty of ways to overcome it.

Most repositories offer scanning and copy services that you can take advantage of in exchange for a small fee. You can also hire a local genealogist to retrieve information for you (visit the Association of Professional Genealogists to find one). Don't overlook the local archives as they may have resources you never knew existed!

STEP 7: ANALYZE YOUR EVIDENCE

Being a genealogist is much like being a lawyer—you're just working in a different time period. You have to be able to prove your conclusion with sound reasoning and reliable sources, otherwise what good is it? Was Aunt Millie really a witness, or did she just overhear some gossip? What about Anthony and Tony—are they the same person, or two different guys? What was great-grandpa's real name ... before he immigrated? You may know the answers to these questions, but can you prove them? That's the question.

I find that it helps to write things out, so that's what I do every time I research. Writing a proof argument helps me analyze the evidence in depth to see if it's credible. It also helps me find discrepancies I never would have seen otherwise. Without analyzing the evidence you find, you can't draw a valid conclusions about what really happened, so try to learn about the different types of evidence there are and how to best use it all. As the saying goes, "Family history without evidence is fiction."

STEP 8: LEARN ABOUT THE GENEALOGICAL GPS

Genealogy has its own set of ethical, moral, and scientific standards, which are collectively known as the GPS (Genealogical Proof Standard). These guidelines were put in place to help you become a better researcher, so visit BCG (Board of Certification for Genealogists) online to start learning about how to research the right way. If it's worth doing, it's worth doing well!

STEP 9: DON'T GIVE UP!

The answer is out there. Somewhere. You just have to find it. I really believe that this is true in the majority of cases, and it's important to not give up even if you can't find an answer at first. A problem like this—one that seems impossible to overcome—is known as a genealogical brick wall. Finding the answers you need can take months, even years, so it's a matter of looking at the problem from different angles to see if you can't spot something that maybe you missed at first glance. Persistence will win out.

If you feel like you can't figure something out on your own, get a fresh take on it from a Professional Genealogist. Two sets of eyes are better than one, and someone with a different perspective might just find something new. Be sure to visit the Association of Professional Genealogists (APG) to find someone with the required knowledge of the local area and time period that can help you through it.

STEP 10: CONNECT WITH OTHER RESEARCHERS

In today's digital society, it's easy to connect with other people who are researching the same areas of your family genealogy and maybe even the same people as you. If you find that this type of detective work is a hobby you enjoy and would like to continue, reach out to other genealogists and learn as much as possible.

In the genealogy world, there are webinars every day of the week, many of which are free, so there's no excuse for not educating yourself. There are hundreds of great blogs you can follow, and plenty of amazing classes you can take. You can even reach out for help on social media. I happen to host a wonderful community that caters to hobby genealogists of Scandinavian heritage, and I know that mine's far from the only one out there.

Whatever niche you're researching, there's a group for that! When you bounce ideas back and forth with others, you're more likely to make progress, so don't be a stranger! Connect! We're all family.

I've known Personal Historian Mary Voell for over ten years and have enjoyed hearing about how she helps her clients preserve their stories in print publication. She has a rich writing style that brings history back to life for her clients; and she knows how important photos and other materials are to saving the past.

THE POWER OF A SINGLE IMAGE
BY MARY VOELL, PERSONAL HISTORIAN

All too often we rely on family photos to tell our cherished stories, photos with faces staring back at us, known and unknown characters, and dates of those whose shoulders we stand upon today. At times, when we look beyond the image, so many stories lie, figuratively and literally, behind those fading faces.

In my role as a personal, family, and organizational historian, I have worked with thousands of images to tell the stories of individuals and families since 2001. I have the opportunity to time travel, to weave my role as storyteller in and through families using family archives and historical documents from global resources alike.

As 21st-century storytellers, we must remember that limiting our narratives to Kodak moments from by-gone eras restricts our ability to tell a fuller, richer story beyond names and dates. When looking at a family photo taken outdoors, have you ever wondered about the weather, the smells, the clothing worn? One client decided to recreate the original recipes of his grandmother's 1850 favorites, then added both to his family publication. Using documents, maps, letters, journals, outside sources, historical context, bits of paper, recipes, and objects adds texture to the history for future readers.

Take for instance, the picture taken of a stained, rusted can handed down through one storyteller's family, allowed the narrator to tell the story of how Grandma saved her pennies for her children's education.

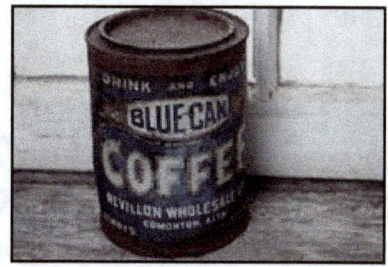

A series of unique and colorful marketing postcards, popular during the early 1900s, were accidently found online and became the seed that allowed the story of a grandparent to unfold beyond the client family's expectations.

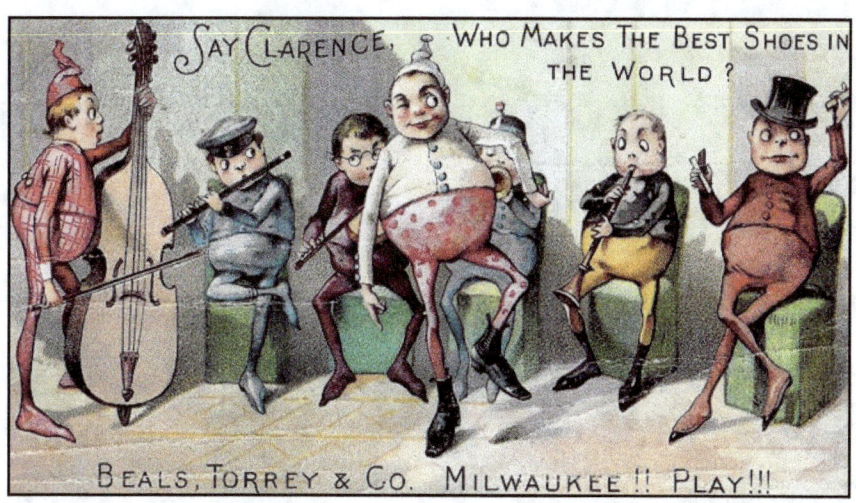

Another treasured image of an 1896 Family Reunion (used with permission) was found in an unopened trunk. The level of organization and the professional presentation tell us of a family that cherished celebrations and delighted in food. One of my favorite sections of this Reunion invitation program is the morning activities:

5:29 ½	Awake from a Peaceful Slumber
5:30	Arise
6:00	Light Refreshments
6:30	Half Hour of Vigorous Exercise
7:00	Bathe
9:30	Arrival
10:00	Distribution of Presents
12:00	Dinner
3:30	Face the Camera

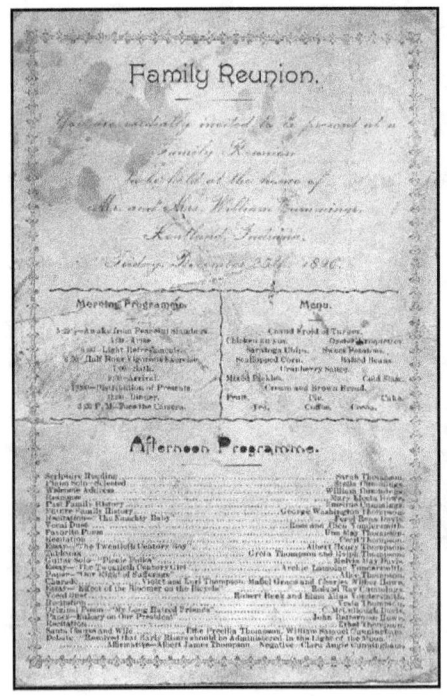

Each generation thinks that it is the only generation that finds exercise or hygiene important, or thinks about how long it took to take a picture of a large family in 1896 for 'Face the Camera', or the family involvement for the afternoon theatrical program. What an absolute treasure.

Another family story is told through the original documentation of the voyages of Captain Cornelius Pratt who sailed the high seas from 1820 to 1842. He departed from the eastern shores of America journeying numerous times to the Mediterranean and across the equator to South America, around Cape Horn to China and the shores of California—long before the Suez Canal was built. An 1849 first-hand account of one such trip, *Reminiscences of a Forty-Niner on a Trip Around the Horn,* was captured by an 18-year-old who dreamt of seeing the world was published in 1912 in the *Grizzly Magazine.* Author William Chessman witnessed vast oceans, the mountains and wildlife of South America, and experienced an on-board mutiny while traveling with Captain Pratt. While no images his adventure are available, the article is reprinted in the family history book, along with maps and thanks to on-line resources, images that paint the picture of a young explorer's experience.

Forty years later, writer William Janz's (*Milwaukee Sentinel* 1984) article wrote of Captain Pratt's great-grandson's day-by-day account of front-line experiences in *Diaries Capture Mood of D-Day.*

While Robert H. Pratt talked of a long-gone war, the diary was in his hand. Forty years ago, Pratt's diary still had pages

Voyages of Captain Cornelius Pratt 1820-1842.

that war would fill; they were the days that preceded the beginning of the end. His involvement in the plans for the largest invasion in the history of the world—5,000 large ships, 4,000 smaller craft, 12,000 planes, 16 million tons of equipment, and hundreds of thousands of men. Americans like Pratt, a lieutenant colonel would land on the beaches of Omaha and Utah in Normandy in the northern part of German -occupied France. The cemeteries are still there to mark what happened that day.

I'm love looking over newspaper articles. The sleuths among us enjoy finding the brief snippets in local newspapers that report visits, travels, babies, accidents—the list is endless. Add them to your narrative. They take your story from dates and names to hobbies and personalities.

These are only a few of the many ways graphic images can embellish your family narrative. As you time-travel through your family photos, organizing, tossing, reorganizing, and digitizing, trying to decide what to do with your original collection, remember to discover, capture and most importantly, preserve the stories behind the images—before It's too late.

In Conclusion

W e have finished going over Pixologie's system for organizing, scanning, and preserving photos. I've shared my approach to genealogy from a layperson's perspective. And, we've touched on dozens of resources that can help you in your family history research.

You have so many different ways to complete and share your work ... Here are some ideas:

- A pedigree chart, perhaps done with calligraphy
- Information entered into a genealogy program that may be shared via a GEDCOM file
- An attractive presentation book
- A story or book about one person, or one line of ancestors
- An article that may be submitted to a genealogical journal
- A booklet to hand out to family members
- A photobook with highlights of the family history
- A traditional genealogy book starting with an immigrant and working forward
- A book of family stories and remembrances of what life was like years ago

- A web page or YouTube video
- An audio story

I truly hope this book has been useful for you in many ways. Here are my last thoughts for you ...

- Enjoy the journey of searching for the people and stories in your family history.
- Don't worry about uncovering every last detail.
- Identify those who have impacted your life in some way today and capture what life was like back then.
- Think about what mattered and what we are taking with us today from the legacy they have left behind.

Thank you so much for allowing me to be a part of your journey in finding, telling, and preserving your family's story.

Keep in touch—I'd love to know if this book has helped and what projects you have completed!

Cheers and blessings,
Mollie Bartelt

mollieb@pixologieinc.com
www.pixologieinc.com

Appendix A: Best Practices for Preserving Your Memories

There are too many options for consumers, too many ways to save a photo, and too little time to figure it out. Over the past two years, at Pixologie, we did a deep dive into developing photo organization standards, digital file format best practices, and levels of service.

I have broken down our best practices into **Preservation** and **Archival levels**. Following these descriptions, I will discuss the **Consumer Level of service**.

Preservation Level

Generally for consumers and family photo collections

- Printed photos are sorted, stored in photo-safe, archival quality boxes

- Scanned photos are 300 or 600 dpi, saved as superior, quality JPGs

- Digital photos are saved as JPGs

- Slides and negatives are scanned at 2000 dpi and saved as JPGs

- Videos and film are transferred to a digital file – MP4

- Back-up includes three digital copies, one onsite (off the main computer) and two offsite

ARCHIVAL LEVEL –

For professional photographers, business and historical photo collections

- Printed photos, slides, negatives are sorted, stored in photo safe, archival quality boxes
- Scanned photos are 600 dpi, saved as TIFFs, once edits completed, can be saved as JPGs
- Digital files are tagged, dates are corrected
- Slides and negatives are scanned at 4000 DPI
- Videos and film are remastered, saved as AVI or MOV
- Back-up includes three digital copies, one onsite (off the main computer) and two offsite

We are committed to educating consumers and our clients on what standards will best preserve their memories for the future.

If you choose a local or online provider to digitize your photos, slides, and other materials, be sure that their digitization settings meet the preservation-level standards listed above.

Appendix B
Notes, Resources & References

Introduction

1) https://www.pewresearch.org/global/2019/02/05/smartphone-ownership-is-growing-rapidly-around-the-world-but-not-always-equally/

2) https://www.sciencedaily.com/releases/2022/02/220224140841.htm

3) https://lifehacker.com/this-chart-shows-how-computer-literate-most-people-are-1789761598

Chapter 1—Why Save Your Family History?

1) https://www.psychologytoday.com/us/blog/the-stories-our-lives/201611/the-do-you-know-20-questions-about-family-stories

Chapter 3—A Quick Primer On What You Might Find

1) *Cycleback, Judging the Authenticity of Photographs*, 5th Edition, 2011, https://tinyurl.com/cyclebackbook

2) https://www.loc.gov/pictures/collection/dag/

3) https://www.loc.gov/rr/print/coll/589_ambrotype.html

4) Maureen Taylor, The Photo Detective https://maureentaylor.com

CHAPTER 4—ORGANIZING THE OLD PHOTOS & DOCUMENTS

1) Pixologie Photo Estate Series
https://www.youtube.com/playlist?
list=PLiPTnYSnq_yjv3smNnjzMjl0zdRvxE8Ll

CHAPTER 5—SCAN THE OLD PHOTOS & DOCUMENTS

1) The International Press Telecommunications Corps –
Photo Metadata website, https://www.iptc.org/
standards/photo-metadata/

2) The Family Metadata History Metadata Working Group on
Facebook (now called savemeta.org), https://
www.facebook.com/groups/3798831010168985 — Request to join the group

CHAPTER 6—PRESERVING THE OLD PHOTOS & DOCUMENTS

1) Archival Methods, www.archivalmethods.com

2) StoryWorth, www.storyworth.com

3) Biograph, https://www.biographbook.com/
Receive 15% off premium subscriptions by emailing
info@biographbook.com with subject: Pixologie Coupon
for Biograph App

CHAPTER 7—ORGANIZING YOUR GENEALOGICAL MATERIALS

1) Number System Resources
https://ancestralfindings.com/genealogical-numbering-
what-is-it-and-how-to-use-it/

Chapter 8—Creating Your Family Tree Online

1) Ancestry, www.ancestry.com

2) FamilySearch, www.familysearch.org

3) https://FamilySearch.org/en/help/helpcenter/article/ find-a-familysearch-center

4) My Heritage, www.myheritage.com

5) Collectionaire, www.collectionaire.com
   Receive 50% off annual subscription – Code: PXFAMILY

Chapter 9—Creating Your Family Tree on Your Computer

1) Family Tree Maker, https://www.mackiev.com/ftm/

2) RootsMagic, https://www.rootsmagic.com

Chapter 10—Websites & Places for Additional Research

1) Ellis Island, https://www.statueofliberty.org/discover/ passenger-ship-search/

   https://www.thoughtco.com/castle-garden-americas-official-immigration-center-1422288

   https://familysearch.org/en/blog/ny-castle-garden-ellis-island

2) Find A Grave, https://www.findagrave.com

3) Newspapers.com, https://www.newspapers.com

4) Fold3, https://www.fold3.com

5) Fire Destroys Military Records, https://
www.archives.gov/personnel-records-center/fire-1973

6) Bureau of Land Management, https://glorecords.blm.gov/
default.aspx

7) Consumer Advocate - Best DNA Testing Based on In-Depth
Reviews, https://www.consumersadvocate.org/dna-
testing

8) RootsTech, https://www.familysearch.org/rootstech

9) Cyndi's List, https://www.cyndislist.com
A comprehensive, categorized, and cross-referenced list of
links that point you to genealogical research sites online.

10) Association of Personal Historians,
https://personalhistorians.org

CHAPTER 11—CLIENT STORIES

1) Polish researcher: Dr. Przemyslaw Jedrzejewski, PhD.
https://yourrootsinpoland.com

CHAPTER 12—COLLEAGUE CONTRIBUTIONS

1) Caroline Guntur, The Swedish Organizer
Email: Caroline@theswedishorganizer.com
Genealogy Website: https://
www.searchingscandinavia.com

2) Mary Voell, Personal Historian. The STORY Expert!
Legacies, LLC | Personal, Family & Organizational Histori-
ans, legaciesstories.com | info@legaciesstories.com
The Making of a Family Historian Classes can be found at
http://legaciesstories.com/classes

About the Author

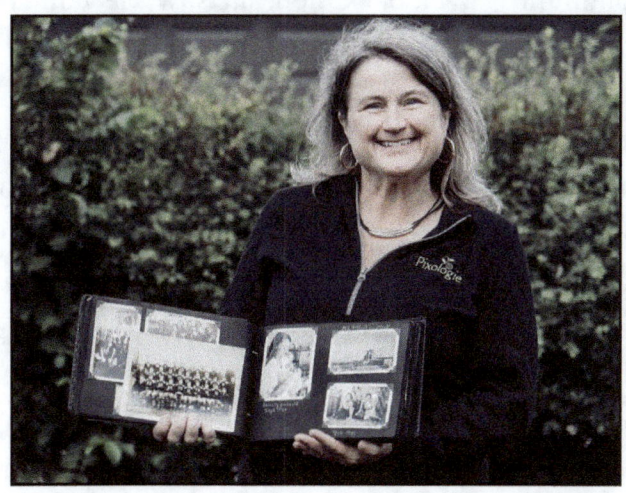

"Take care of all your memories, for you cannot relive them."

—Bob Dylan

This quote describes why Mollie Bartelt is so passionate about saving family photos. She often says, "If I don't have a photo of a memory, I don't remember it happening!"

Life is flying by and Mollie knows personally that people are in danger of losing important family moments. We all need to pause from hectic lifestyles to reflect on how our photos are being saved to enjoy today, tomorrow and for future generations.

Mollie's career began in the nonprofit, health care and assisted living fields, where she ran adult day centers and other community programs to help older adults remain living in the community. Even back then, she saw the value of family photographs and photo albums as a comfort and memory tool for her clients.

Along the way, Mollie married Paul and they had two children named Hannah and Alex. During that time, she loved scrapbooking for her family to enjoy looking through and seeing all the family had done together. She began selling Creative Memories albums and digital photo book software. Here, she met Ann Matuszak, who became her friend and future business partner.

Both Ann and Mollie, along with their other friends in the business, were very disappointed when Creative Memories went into bankruptcy for the second time in 2013. Ann had an idea of starting a photo organizing business and Mollie was hooked on the idea because she knew people needed hands-on help organizing and scanning photos.

They launched Pixologie in July of 2013 and it quickly went far beyond a home-based business. Mollie and Ann opened their first location in 2014. They were semi-finalists in the 2017 Wisconsin Governor's Business Plan Contest and were awarded Small Business of the Year by the South Suburban Chamber of Commerce in the beginning of 2020. They began offering "photo estate" services to help families preserve their collections to enjoy today and pass on to future generations.

With the pandemic, many changes came to Pixologie. They began putting educational videos and reviews up on YouTube because of the shutdown. At the end of 2020, the business downsized and Mollie became the sole owner.

Today, Pixologie continues to provide photo estate and digitization services in Southeastern Wisconsin. In addition, Mollie works with people around the country and the world helping them figure out their photo organizing challenges and providing a system to save photos. Her signature program, The Pix Plan Course and Community, provides motivation, education, and inspiration to help people enjoy saving their memories once and for all.

Need help? Schedule a complimentary appointment with Mollie here:

www.calendly.com/mollieb/pixplan

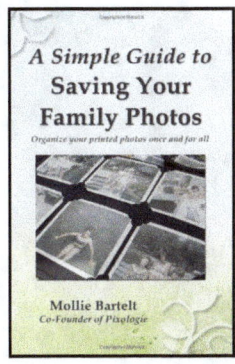 A Simple Guide to Saving Your Family Photos
(September 5, 2016)

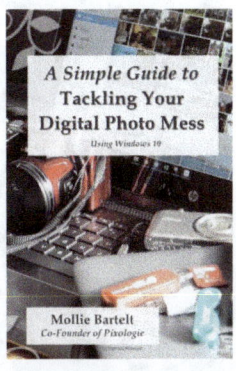 A Simple Guide to Tackling Your Digital Photo Mess: Using Windows 10 (April 19, 2017

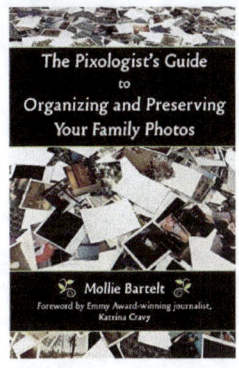 The Pixologist's Guide to Organizing and Preserving Your Family Photos
(November 1, 2018)

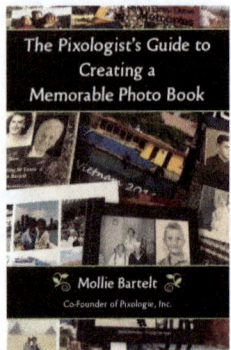 The Pixologist's Guide to Creating a Memorable Photo Book (March 1, 2019)

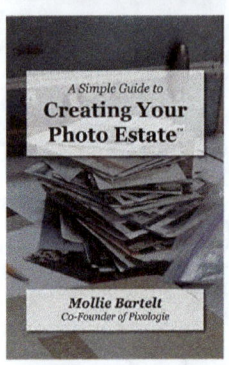 A Simple Guide to Creating a Photo Estate (January 31, 2020)

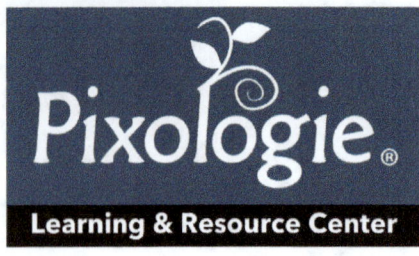 For more education and support, visit www.thepixplan.com